# *Remembering Mama*
## *God's Faithful Servant*

*"…I urge you to live a life worthy of the calling
you have received.
Be completely humble and gentle; be patient,
bearing with one another in love."
Eph. 4: 1-2 NIV*

## *by Kathleen Kennedy*

ELITE

www.xulonpress.com

This book is dedicated to all who contributed

to my journey of learning:

Mama and Papa,

sisters and brothers:

Margaret, Olivia, Margery, Evadne, John,

Cynthia, and Eric;

in-laws Debbie and Earl and

Matthew and Johnnel;


daughters Elyse and Vanessa,

grandsons Micah and Noah;


teachers of St. Isabella School of Bermudian

Landing,

Ms. Ellen Baptist and Mrs. Laurine Pook;

and to Godly women everywhere,
including my dearest friends Ms. Marva,
Pipsi, Ivy, Therese,
and Linda (RIP),

my nieces and nephews in Belize and America –

May the good Lord bless and keep you
as you continue in the things which you have
learned and
have been assured of, knowing of whom you have
learned them.

# Introduction

Mama grew up in Ashford, a small village located about thirty miles west of the old capital. She was the second daughter born to David and Agnes Fitzgerald and the third of nine children.

Those were the days when children were blessings from God. They were respectful, obedient, and kind. They worked side by side with their parents. Everyone worked. Why? If they didn't work, they didn't eat. There was no such thing as a hand out or welfare from the government.

When parents could no longer work, their children took care of them. There were no retirement homes, no convalescent homes. Many people died in the very home in which they were born.

People believed in a higher Authority. They took care of each other. They worked hard. Raising cattle and tilling the soil was hard work but it was the way of life.

And everyone in Mama's home read the Bible every single day.

Papa was from a village in the Northern part of the country. He grew up on a farm and planted watermelons, avocados, plantains, and bananas. Papa was no rancher, and he never hunted or fished. Other men fished and hunted, then walked from village to village or sent their children to sell their catch: 10 cents for a pound of fish; 25 cents a pound for deer meat.

Papa was a very independent man. He didn't socialize much. He went to no one's home and only a selected few visited his home when he was around. Papa was blessed with eight children and he worked us from before the sun rose until after the sun set. If it were left to him, we would have spent our lives working on the plantation. I am not sure if he would have allowed us to go to school.

Most of Papa's family resided in the old capital city. Until I moved to the city, I knew his brothers and sisters by name only; in fact, I have never met his eldest sister. She is the only surviving sibling and she still resides in the village where she was born.

I don't know much about Papa nor his side of the family. In our home, an invisible line separated parents and children. There wasn't much conversation about families. Children followed directions, worked hard, and studied their lessons. Parents provided shelter, food, and clothing (with the assistance of children).

My parents were married in 1950. Mama was 25 and Papa 30. For the first four years of their marriage, they lived about five miles from my maternal grandparents. Then they moved to Langley, a village located about 26 miles west of the old capital and about ten miles north east of where my maternal grandparents lived. When they moved, Mama received several heads of cattle from her parents. Papa purchased 27 acres of land but he allowed the government to build a road through the property dividing it into 10 acres on one side and 17 on the other. In addition, he rented an additional fifty acres to keep the cattle and horses and cut plantations.

Papa cut plantation on a rotation basis between the fifty acres and land across the river. There were acres and acres of uninhabited, undeveloped land across the river from the village. Those were the days when farmers showed up, marked out the acreage they wanted to farm that year, and chopped their plantation.

Every two years or so, we traveled across the river to cut plantation. When I was little, Papa carried me on his back while Mama carried Melanie who was two years younger than me. We left early in the morning while it was still dark, went down to the banks of the river, climbed in the dowry, and paddled to the plantation which was about three miles away. After disembarking, my sister and I were carried another two miles from the river to the actual site to be cultivated. Upon arrival, I was placed under a tree to watch my little sister, while my parents chopped, planted, weeded, or harvested. We returned home about 11 A.M. While Papa napped under the house, Mama had no time to snooze. First, she picked in the clothes off the line that she had washed earlier that morning, then prepared dinner (lunch in America).

While our property was surrounded with a barbed-wire fence, most villagers did not fence in theirs. However, everyone knew where one property line ended and the other began. Our house was in the middle of seventeen acres and the land was cleared so that I could sit on the steps and see the outside activities of the neighbors to my right and left. Across the road, about five hundred yards in front of me, was the sporting field with enough space to house the Saturday activities: cricket, football (soccer), softball, and the beginning and ending of horse races. Since I couldn't attend the festivities, I sat on the steps, peered out into the distance, and tried to catch a glimpse of participants and spectators.

Having a two-storey house was a necessity. The living quarters were upstairs and underneath was empty, for a reason. Papa piled up several pieces of board there and we sat on them during the day and enjoyed the breeze. It was also a place to study and nap during the day. When people passed through from other villages, it was a place to sit, drink a glass of water, and enjoy a few minutes of rest. In addition, it housed the clothes line during the rainy season. Laundry had to be done daily, because we did not have more than three sets of clothing at any one time.

In the villages, the kitchen was never attached to the house. As I grew up, I discovered why. If there was a fire in the kitchen, it would burn down and take the house with it. There was no fire department and no one had even heard of a telephone. By separating the kitchen from the house, the latter would be spared during a fire. During my early years, fire destroyed two houses in my village and people watched them burned; one was arson.

Religion was very important to the villagers. Most were Catholic and about 2 percent, Anglicans. Adventists made up less than half of one percent of the population. Mama was Anglican. The pastor showed up once a month and met with his congregation in a village located two miles from where we lived. That was too far for Mama to walk especially during inclement weather.

Papa was Catholic, in name only, but all his children had to be baptized Catholic. The priest came to the village once a month and Mama accompanied us to Mass. There wasn't a church building so Mass was held in the larger of the two classrooms. There were no crying babies in church, nor were there any nurseries. There were no bathrooms either so members of the congregation could not disturb others by walking to and fro.

Mama sat with us for the three-hour service. There was Confession before Mass and even before we were eligible for Confession and Communion, we all showed up and sat and prayed silently in church until the priest moved from behind the confessional. We never left the pew, except for Confession and Communion. We sat quietly during the Homily but participated in the rest of the Mass either standing or kneeling (on the cement floor). No one complained about the hard floor; that was all we knew.

I got a whipping once for taking Communion before I had officially received the Sacrament of Holy Communion. I always wanted to taste that white, round thing that looked like a wafer. To receive the Sacrament, eligible participants filed up and kneeled in front of the first row of benches to receive the 'host.' So one Sunday, before my First Holy Communion, I sat in the front row, slid out of my seat, knelt without drawing attention (so I thought), and received the 'host.' When we returned home, Melanie lodged a complaint and I received a whipping for 'making a mockery' of the Sacrament.

I still remember kissing Bishop Hodap's ring at Confirmation (the Sacrament that followed First Holy Communion). Before the Confirmation ceremony, participants occupied the front two rows. Bishop Hodap was the teacher. He asked lots of questions about the Bible and the various Sacraments. I was the first to raise my hand and I had the right answers. As a reward, I got to kiss his ring. Yes, that was a big deal.

Growing up, I took everything in church very seriously. It was a place to be reverent. There was plenty of praying and lots of singing. We did not have any musical accompaniment but I always left Mass singing or humming. I really felt something magical when I left Mass.

Catholics experienced several changes after the Vatican II Conference in the early sixties. Before Vatican II, Mass was in Latin and the priest had his back to the congregation. Just prior to giving Communion to the faithful, the priest held up this huge 'host'. It was probably six inches in diameter. I actually believed that all the little hosts somehow, magically came from that big one. The changes at the Conference enlightened me. The first time the priest faced the audience, I noticed that all the little hosts were in the chalice. I was shocked. How could Christ's body be in those little hosts? And what about the blood of Christ? At that time, the Congregation was not given wine; only the priest drank from the wine chalice. Was the priest really drinking the blood of Christ?

Mama knows the Bible. It's her Book of Standards. She reads it every day, rain or shine, during good times or bad. She believes every word. She follows the teachings of Christ and preaches them. She has never questioned anything in the Bible. And regardless of the topic, she always recites the appropriate Bible verses during a conversation.

Mama taught her children to read and write before they started school. Beginning with her first child, Mama demonstrated that learning was important. When Mama finished her daily chores, usually after dinner, she pulled out books from her childhood and taught me to read using phonetic strategies. If I didn't know the word, Mama would say, "Spell the word." After I spelled it, she'd say "Sound it out in pieces." After telling me the word, Mama would have me 'repeat' it, 'spell' it, then 'say' it again. I had to read paragraph by paragraph without making mistakes. Any mistake resulted in rereading from the beginning of the story.

Reading was followed with writing. Mama wrote words on a slate and I copied them, then, read them to her. Mama never learned to print, so I learned to write in cursive at an early age. '*Chicken scratch*' was not acceptable, so my writing had to be perfect.

The back cover of the exercise books (notebooks) was filled with mathematic tables. The first tables I memorized were multiplication facts, from two times one is two to two times twelve equals 24. As soon as I memorized the twos, it was on to the threes, and so on until I got to twelve times twelve equals 144. It was more difficult when Mama combined multiplication with division facts. For example, two times one is two, two into two one. Imagine doing this all the way to 12 times 12 is 144; 144 divided by 12 is

12. It didn't matter to her that "the teacher wasn't there yet."

While I studied, Melanie sat nearby in a carton box. She took in the information because she blurted out words that I had previously recited. When Mama was convinced that I could study on my own, she got me started on a lesson, then, spent time with Melanie. Pretty soon, I became Melanie's teacher. I conducted my own classes on Saturdays. I was the teacher; my sister, the pupil. As the other siblings came along, Saturday was school day in our house. I looked forward to Saturdays because I got to be the Principal. During the week, that was Mama's job.

After school work, it was Bible-reading time. Mama chose the passages and we read them. Then she assigned memory verses that had to be memorized and recited within minutes.

There was no kindergarten. Primary School included the following: Infants I and II, followed by Standards I to VI. Upon the completion of Standard VI (Grade 8), all students took the Primary School

Examination. To prevent cheating, this examination was administered in the city. Students from the villages were assigned to schools throughout the city. Students who attended schools in the city took the exam in a school other than their home school. Passing this exam meant that the student had successfully completed Primary School and was eligible for Secondary School, also known as High School.

To attend any of the three Catholic high schools, students had to pass the High School Entrance Examination. Boys would be eligible for St. Ignatius's College; girls had a choice of either St. Mary's Academy or St. Agatha's High School. The only requirement to attend non-Catholic high schools was completing primary school. Regardless of religious affiliation, students could attend any school they chose. Tuition was required for all post-primary school education.

I passed the high school entrance and the primary school exams on my first try. I was 12 years old. Papa wanted me to go to St. Mary's Academy but Sister Vasquez, the principal, had other ideas. I can still remember our first visit with her. "This child is too young. Have her go back to primary school for another year," she commanded. It was back to primary school and farming for another year, but I didn't mind. I had plenty of growing up to do.

Papa could have sent me to a non-Catholic high school, but he wanted me to go to St. Mary's because he knew some of the nuns there, especially Sister Mary, the school's namesake. When he was a little boy, he used his dowry to transport her and other nuns from village to village as they spread the Word of God.

Whether it was teaching from the Bible or textbooks, Mama prepared us for the future. We had to do things the right way. She always asked this question, "Would Jesus be pleased with your words and deeds?"

Mama raised her children and grandchildren the way her Mother raised her. I have to admit that being a working mother outside the home did not afford me the luxury of spending quality time with my children. Even though I explained to her, that in America, I have to put in the time to move up the corporate ladder, Mama let me know that she was not pleased with my priority – putting my job ahead of my family.

Although she has changed countries, Mama has not given up her core values. She continues to read her Bible every day and to live each day as if it's her last.

## To Mama with Love

O Mama, thank you for everything.

Thank you for being my mother.

God knew what He was doing when He created you,

His faithful servant to lead the rest.

You fed the hungry

and encouraged the weary.

You nurtured the sick

and cared for the weak when all seemed

bleak,

You loved the loveless

and sheltered the homeless

because the Bible told you so.

Mama, you worked hard all your life

    and you never complained.

You ended the day the same way you began

    praying to the Father who created you.

You were never ashamed of Him

    And daily you proclaimed, "I am His faithful

    servant."

You trusted in Him, you worshipped Him,

You adored Him, you praised him,

You rejoiced in His mercy.

And as a reward

Your Father waived three score and ten

And gave you over four score and more

Then said, "Welcome home, my faithful servant."

"For what profit is it to a man if he gains the whole world, and loses his own soul? Or what will a man give in exchange for his soul?"

Mt. 16:26 NKJV

It was a cool, breezy Friday afternoon. My daughter and I were spending a few days with Mama who lives about a two-hour drive north from our home. Mama and I chatted in the kitchen while my daughter watched television. Suddenly, my daughter announced, "He died."

"Who died?" I asked.

She pointed to the television screen. Mama and I moved over to the den. A well-known television personality had died suddenly in his Washington Office.

We listened for two hours to all the accolades from colleagues, employees, and politicians. Someone mentioned the homes he owned which prompted this comment from Mama, "I haven't heard anything about him being a Christian. He can't take any of that stuff with him. What does it profit a man if he gains the whole world and loses his soul?"

As we listened to the commentators and reporters, someone finally mentioned that the man was Catholic and strongly believed in his faith, which prompted this response from Mama, "I bet not one of them is saved. Not one of them talked about being saved. All this means nothing. The day of judgment will come..."

"But Mama, this is not about any of them. This is about..."

"The Bible says, 'Whosoever believeth in Him should not perish but have everlasting life.'"

I decided it was time to tell Mama's story.

"For even when we were with you, we gave you
this rule:
'If a man will not work, he shall not eat.'"
2 Thess. 3:10 NIV

"**M**ama, what was life like when you were growing up?"

"It was not easy. We were up at three in the morning. Every one of us had something to do. We were told once and we took care of business: floors swept, clothes washed and hung on the line, cows milked, and plantation cut. Crops were planted, weeded, or harvested. We went down to the river, bathed, and got ready for school."

"Who determined which chore each child received?"

"Mum (her mother) did. Most of the time, when we were not in school, the girls stayed home with her. We learned from each other. We did the house work: washed, cooked, and cleaned, while the boys were with Pop (her father). They hunted game, tended cattle, and farmed the land. They cut and weeded the plantation. We helped them with the harvesting of the crops on Saturdays and during breaks from school."

"Your family owned lots of cattle and farmland. Did your father hire additional workers?"

"No, family members were the non-paid, hired help. People who were less fortunate stopped by and helped out for a day's meal. When one farmer was finished with his chores, he took his boys to help another. No one had to ask for help. You helped one another. People believed in working together."

"Did everyone live near the river?"

"Most people built their homes near the banks of the river but they allowed space for the water to rise, especially during the floods when the river overflowed its bank. The horses, cows, sheep, pigs, chickens, and turkeys needed water. People needed water to wash, cook, and clean. You did not want to carry buckets of water from afar."

"How did you survive without a washer and dryer and no electricity?"

"True, there was no electricity in the villages and there wasn't much in the city either. At night, we used kerosene lamps. In those days, no one had ever heard of a washer and dryer. My father made wash bowls out of mahogany or whatever wood held water. We filled the bowls with water from the river and washed every day. We scrubbed the clothes with our hands, then, rinsed and hung them on the clothes line. "

"Was there anyone who washed clothes in the river?"

"Yes, a few of the women did, but we were close enough that we carried the water and washed closer to the lines."

"Were all the girls washing?"

"No, depending on age, we rotated the cleaning, washing, and cooking every week. However, when we were finished with our assigned job, we did not sit idly by. We helped someone else. That's how we were raised. Everyone worked together."

"You didn't have a stove either."

"That's true. There was no stove but who needed one? We had a huge fire hearth. You built as many fires as needed for the number of pots being used."

"Who cut the firewood?"

"The boys did but when they were busy out in the fields, the girls handled that."

"The boys had their hands full."

"Yes, they had plenty to do on the ranch. After a calf was born, they had to dress the navel. Sometimes worms would get into it and that required plenty of attention. They made sure that all of the cattle were accounted for and hunted for the strays. Branding the animals did not prevent them from getting lost."

"How many calves were born each week?"

"There was at least one new-born a week."

"I remember having to dress the navel, too. It was awful."

"There were no animal doctors, so we learned how to do things. Everything was handed down from generation to generation. Even the girls roped and cared for the calves."

"It sure was a family affair. Mama, let's talk about farming. What did you plant and who did what?"

"Pop was in the fields with the boys. Sometimes, other young men from neighboring villages showed up. Everyone within five square miles knew that there would be food at our house, so they showed up and pitched in where they were needed; but mostly, Pop and my brothers worked the fields. The girls helped on Saturdays and when we were out of school. Depending on what needed to be done, the girls helped with the planting, weeding, and harvesting.

"On the plantation, we planted rice and corn; different kinds of beans: red kidney, pinto, and lima; cocoa, cassava, sweet potato, yam, pumpkin, and squash; plantain, banana, and sugarcane. Closer to the house, there was pineapple, mango, orange, grapefruit, sweet lime, lemon, plum, and tomato. We planted plenty of spices: thyme, bud pepper, mint. You name it, we planted it."

"You didn't have to buy much from the stores, did you?"

"Not really. We made molasses and syrup from sugarcane. We milked our cows, churned butter, and made cheese. We even made cooking oil and soap. About once every three months, Pop would catch the boat and go to the city to buy what we couldn't make. There weren't any stores in the villages."

"Those were the days when boats were the limousines of transportation."

"Yes, people traveled by boat. Once a month, a boat transported people from the villages to the city. The journey lasted one to two days, depending on the weather. We knew the day when the boat came, so Pop waited along the banks of the river and got picked up. During the floods, there was no boat. It was too dangerous."

"What did Pop buy in the city?"

"He bought flour, salt, black pepper that we had to grind, nutmeg that we had to grate, and cloth that we had to sew. We didn't buy 'ready-made' things. Mum taught us all to sew, by hand. We sewed table cloths, sheets, curtains, pillow cases, dresses, shirts, pants, and undergarments – whatever we needed. It's not like we had tons of clothing to sew. We only needed three sets of clothes. That's why we washed every day. There was a set for Sunday; that's your Sunday best. Later on, Mum bought a sewing machine. She taught us how to use it, but that did not replace sewing by hand."

"I remember having three sets of clothes and sewing on my hand. If I didn't sew it right, you made me rip out the stitches and re-stitch again. Machine stitches were the most difficult because you wanted the job to look as though it was sewn on a machine. Now I buy rather than sew."

"Yes, you bought all these clothes and shoes. Look around this room. You don't need all this stuff.

Remember, we brought nothing into this world, and we take nothing out. I would rather have Jesus that anything this world affords today."

"Maybe, I am making up for what I didn't have." Mama gave me that look, so I continued, "Mama, things are different here. You didn't have to pay for water, gas, electricity, sewer, and garbage. I do; consequently, I can't wash and cook every day. Plus, I work out in public. Imagine wearing the same outfit every other day."

"Is it cleaned and pressed? We had to heat our irons over the fire in order to iron. Now you just plug it in a socket. You have it too easy."

It was time to change the subject. "I understand that Saturday was a full day for everyone."

"Saturdays were our busiest days when school was in session. This is the day for churning butter, and making molasses, soap, and cooking oil. We did all the work that was too big to handle during the week."

"You taught me how to make cooking oil. That's an all-day job."

"Yes, it is. On the plantation, we piled up cohunes for when we needed them. Then on Saturdays, we broke the shells and removed the nuts."

"That was the easy part."

"Next, put the nuts in a mortar and beat them with the mortar stick." The mortar was hewn from wood. It was about four feet tall and resembled a barrel. Dig out just enough wood to shape the inside like a cone. It has to be about two feet deep so the contents will not jump out when beaten.

"I hated the beating. My hands were very sore at the end of the day."

"The finer the texture, the more oil we got. Beat the nuts as close to powder-form as possible. Then put water in a drum, about three-fourths full of water, build a huge fire under it, put in the contents from the mortar and let it boil for about three hours, long enough until the oil floats on top of the water. Based on experience, we know how much oil we should get from the amount of nuts beaten."

"But that's not the end?"

"No, skim the oil off the water and put it into a pot on the fire hearth. Let it fry until all the water has been removed. It's finished when it's quiet in the pot - there is no popping sound coming from the water. Remove it from the fire and let it cool. The following morning, bottle it and it's ready for cooking and baking."

"It's obvious that you are used to hard work."

"I did not see what we did as hard work. There was no handout. If we didn't work, we didn't eat. We did not dare sit around while others worked. We knew what needed to be done, so we pitched in. The Bible says, 'By the sweat of thy brow thou shall eat bread,' and 'all hard work bringeth a profit.'"

"Pastor Jay (Jay Pankratz, Senior Pastor at Sunrise Church in Rialto) preached a sermon on 'Faith in the Family.' He shared several verses that related to work. All lazy people should have heard him. You would have enjoyed the message because you have been saying the same words as far back as I can remember. 'Work for what you want and take care of your family and whatsoever thy hand findeth to do, do it with thy might; for there is no work, nor device, nor knowledge, nor wisdom, in the grave, whither thou goest.'"

"Read your Bible every day and do what it tells you."

"Yes Ma'am."

"Not that I speak in respect of want:
for I have learned, in whatsoever state I am,
therewith to be content." Phil. 4:11 KJV

"**M**ama, tell me about your schooling."
"We walked five miles to school every day, rain or shine. When we got to school, we went down to the river and washed our feet and put on our shoes. We were never late. We started school at age five, but when we turned fourteen, we had to leave. Most of us reached Standard Six *(grade eight in America)*.

"The school had one room and one teacher. Children were obedient and respectful. While the teacher worked with one group, the rest did their work. When the older ones were finished, they helped the younger ones. If we misbehaved, the teacher whipped us. If word got back to our parents, we got another whipping. Everyone behaved because we did not want to disgrace our family."

"'We did not want to disgrace our family.' If only the children of today learned those words. You wouldn't believe how students today abused their teachers. They cursed them out; some used words I have never heard before. Others assault their teachers. Two male students at my high school slugged the teacher but the principal did not want him to file a police report. I recently learned of a first grader who slapped her teacher. Just today, one of my ninth grade girls wrote a note that she would kill me. She put her name on it and passed it around and not one student said a word. The last student who read the note, left it on her desk."

"Where are the parents?"

"Mama, some of the parents are worst than the children; most cannot even control their children. Do you know some children actually beat their parents?"

"Why don't the parents call the police?"

"They are afraid of their children, and some are illegal immigrants. Anyway, I am glad you raised us to understand that 'disgracing the family was not an option.' Now, walking five miles to school? I can't imagine…"

"Then how will you get to school?"

"Ride a horse."

"Walking didn't kill anyone."

It was time to change channels. "What did you study in school?"

"Reading, writing, and arithmetic - we learned how to read correctly – not to read like someone is chasing you. We had to write neatly – no chicken scratch. We memorized our multiplication tables."

"You mentioned that you had to leave school at age 14."

"Yes, we had to make room for younger children. So we took advantage of the time we had in school."

"Who paid the teacher?"

"Families sent chickens, eggs, meat, rice, and corn – whatever they had. The same teacher was at our school for over fifteen years. I don't know if he was paid by the Government."

"You mentioned meat. Where did it come from?"

"Men hunted deer and other small games. Fishing was also important and different kinds of fishes were found in different areas of the river. That meant a couple days from home to set nets or to fish. Every three months or so, we slaughtered a cow. That was another all day job. All hands were needed and nothing was wasted."

"There was no refrigerator and you couldn't cook all the meat in one day..."

"That's true but planning was the key. Most of the meat was smoked. The parts that we didn't smoke, we cooked right away: heart, kidney, liver, tongue, feet. We shared the meat with our neighbors who were about three to five miles down the river. We always shared."

"I know that. You haven't stop."

"The Bible says to be generous and be willing to share."

"What happened after you left school?"

"Girls helped with the chores in the home while the boys worked on the ranch."

"Do you know anyone who left the village and moved to the city for higher education?"

"I attended primary school with students from three neighboring villages because each village did not have a school. Once we finished Standard Six, I seldom saw the students again. From time to time when I went into the city, I ran into a former class-mate who was working. I don't remember anyone from my village who went on to college. Everyone was needed on the farm. College was mostly reserved for city children, but I am grateful to my parents for letting me stay in school so that I could learn how to read and write."

"I cannot imagine how people can survive without being literate, but some do. Recently, I heard about a father who learned to read after his two daughters got married and left home."

"When I was growing up, going to school was mandatory. When we got there, we studied and did our lessons or the teacher whipped us. So we all tried."

"Nowadays, it's different. Some parents have no idea what literacy means. They cannot read or write, nor speak English, and they do not push their children to learn. Children spend their time watching television or hanging out with their friends. Things would be a lot better if there was no welfare system and people had to work, whether it was in the fields or along the freeway. Children need to see that if they didn't work, they wouldn't eat."

"Is getting rid of welfare the answer?"

"It's a start but it will never happen. Mama, you wouldn't believe the hue and cry that would follow the suggestion for the abolition of welfare: 'How can you starve the children? It's not fair. You are violating our constitutional rights…'"

"Is welfare in the Constitution?"

"No Ma'am, but they use the Constitution as a crutch." After pausing awhile, I had to ask, "Were you contented with having to leave school to work on a farm?"

"That was all I knew. My parents expected help from me." After thinking a moment, Mama continued, "Yes, I was contented. I worked very hard. There were no handouts. I was contented with what I had. Today, I am still contented. Like Paul, I have learned to be contented whatever the circumstances. I have had a full plate and an empty one. My Father giveth me strength and I can do anything through Him."

"If you could do it all over again, what would you change?"

"Nothing. I would not change a thing. I had good parents, good brothers, good sisters. I lived a good life. I am contented. The Bible says, 'Trust in the

Lord with all thine heart and lean not unto thine own understanding. In all thy ways acknowledge him, and he shall direct thy paths.'"

"For six days, work is to be done, but the
seventh day is a Sabbath of rest, holy to
the Lord." Ex. 31:15a NIV

"Now that you have slaved all week, I bet
you were happy when Sunday came.
Mama, what did you do on Sundays?"

"We got up early, washed and cooked. The idea
was that even though it was Sunday, if you got the
chores done before the rising of the sun, you were
observing the Sabbath. Afterward, we all went to
church. Sometimes we rode horses to church, but
not often. The service was held in the one-room
school house. The teacher led the praying, singing,
and reading of the Bible. We didn't have a choir or

any musical instrument. If we were lucky, the pastor from the city showed up once a year. After church, we returned home, ate, and spent the rest of the day resting and reading the Bible."

"Talk about the influence of the Bible in your life."

"We grew up in a God-fearing home. Every word we uttered, every deed we performed – we knew that we would be held accountable, not only to our parents, but to God. The Bible says, 'whatsoever thou doest, whether in word or deed, do it all in the name of the Lord Jesus.' My parents made sure that we followed the teachings of Christ."

"What was your religion?"

"Anglican."

"There were times when you didn't go to church because of the weather…"

"True, but that didn't stop us from worshipping God at home. We had our own service."

"Who led the group?"

"Mum did. We had our own choir."

"I have heard you and Aunt Vicky (Mama's youngest sister) sing. You ladies can bring it. I can imagine how the family choir sounded. These hymns that you sing remind me of the summer revivals back in the fifties. People met for a whole week every summer praising God and singing. They showed up from a ten-square mile radius. Most came in the evenings, stayed until 10 P.M. then returned home after the services, only to return the next day. Those were the good days.

"I have to ask this question. Was there ever a time when one of you said, 'I don't feel like praying or reading the Bible today. I worked all week and I am just going to kick back.'"

"Excuse me? We were respectful children. The Bible says, 'Honor thy father and thy mother that thy days may be long lived upon the land which the Lord thy God giveth thee.' There were no arguments in our house. Every one respected each other."

"There wasn't much else to do any way."

"There was no radio or television, for sure. There were no movies or parties. After we did our chores, we were allowed to visit a relative. Again, that person may be five miles away. So it was better if we relaxed with our Bible because Monday was a work day. The Bible says, 'Great peace have they which love thy law, and nothing shall offend them.'"

"Let's go back to the singing in your home. What was one of your favorites?"

Mama began to sing,

> I hear the Savior say,
> "Thy strength indeed is small
> Child of weakness watch and pray,
> Find in Me thine all in all."
>
> Jesus paid it all,
> All to Him I owe,
> Sin had left a crimson stain
> He washed it white as snow.

"Teach me your way, O Lord, and I will
walk in your truth." Ps. 86:11a NIV

"**M**ama, not a day goes by that you
don't read the Bible. Ever since I can
remember, you have been reading the Bible and
quoting scriptures to us. Why?"

"The Bible tells me to pray without ceasing and
give thanks to God. I have to do this every day. I
read the Bible and give God the glory. You need to
live right and I want you all to know that you have
to follow God's commandments. I am supposed to
teach you, lead by example, help you to develop good
character, and learn responsibility. There will come a
day when I have to give account of my actions. As a

parent, my job is to teach you what is right and make sure you do it."

"I can remember all those beatings we got. Thank goodness we weren't raised in America."

"The Bible says, 'Discipline your son and he will give you peace. Do not spare the rod and spoil the child. Train up a child the way he should go and when he is old he will not depart from it. The rod and reproof giveth wisdom, but a child left to himself bringeth his mother shame.' Look at the world today. Children have no respect for their parents or anyone else. Look at all the crimes. If people read their bibles and follow God's teachings, do you think there would be all these problems? You cannot say that I did not teach you to do what is right."

"No, Ma'am, I wouldn't dare. Mama, has it ever crossed your mind that the Bible may have been written by men who used events in history to scare their followers into doing the right thing? I listen to some preachers today and I know for a fact they make up some of the things they say just for effect or to scare people into compliance, like Jonathan Edwards did. I believe that the prophets were creative, too."

"Gloria, God guided the prophets and others to write down His words so that we may follow them. We cannot enter Heaven as sinners. We have to accept Christ and believe that He died for us; then, follow His examples. I believe in this Book (Mama held up the Bible) and I don't want to hear that nonsense."

"Yes, Ma'am, but I have one more question on the topic. Do you believe that there is a Heaven and Hell? Sometimes, I believe that Heaven and Hell are right here on Earth."

"Get your Bible and read it. The Bible says, 'Wait for His Son from Heaven. You will enter the kingdom of Heaven if you doeth the will of my Father who is in Heaven. My kingdom is not of this world. I go to prepare a place for you. Henceforth there is laid up for me a crown of righteousness, which the Lord, the righteous judge, shall give me at that day.' Yes, there is a Heaven and it's not here.

"And the Bible tells us that there is a Hell. Remember the story of the rich man and Lazarus? 'In Hell, where he was tormented, he looked up and saw Abraham far away.' Yes, there is a Hell and it's not here on Earth. Go and read your Bible. In this house we will read and believe."

"Yes Ma'am." It was time for me to collect my thoughts.

"… and why am I depriving myself of enjoyment." Eccles.. 4:8c NIV

The word "enjoyment" was not in our vocabulary. Mama intentionally missed this verse in her Bible. On Saturdays, other children accompanied their parents to cricket matches, horse racing, or birthday parties. In my house, we swept the yard, washed clothes, scrubbed the fire hearth and floors, and cooked dinner (when we weren't slaving on the plantation). Afterward, we gathered our 'lessons' and moved underneath the house to study. The last book read was the Bible. This was to get us ready for Sunday.

Something happened when I was about six years old. Our house was about 400 yards from the gate; yet, I could see directly out the gate and down the road to the school, which was less than a mile away. It was a Saturday evening. I had finished my 'lessons' and was still sitting underneath the house. Four of my classmates, walked through the gate, holding hands. Mama must have seen them and she stood at the top of stairs. It was about 14 steps to the top.

"Ms. Middleton, can Gloria come with us to my birthday party?"

"Gloria isn't going to any birthday party. She has lessons to do."

My classmates turned around and left. I was never invited to anything else by anyone. I have always wondered why we had to stay home and study while other children were out and about enjoying themselves. Unless it was a school activity, we did not participate.

"Train up a child in the way he should go:
and when he is old, he will not depart
from it." Prov.22:6 KJV

I started school in a one-room hut. The dirt floor was easy to sweep. Students took turns cleaning the school on Friday afternoons. Class sizes were small; very few exceeded six students. There was an advantage to being in one room. You could see and hear what was happening in all the classes. And you were learning.

Rules and consequences were never posted in the classroom. In fact, there was nothing on the wall, not even a blackboard. Students worked from their workbooks. Children were trained at home to respect authority. They had to behave at home and in public. Teachers were allowed to whip children at school. Neighbors also had that authority. Children knew that complaints regarding their unacceptable behaviors, if relayed to their home, would result in dire consequences. It was all about the 'family with good children.'

I don't remember much of my first two years in school. Miss Baptist was my teacher and the principal was Mr. Arana. He came from the Southern part of the country. His mother was bitten by a poisonous snake. Every day after school, Mama would take me to visit her. I couldn't figure out why but members of other families from the village showed up to help out around the home. The 'snake man' couldn't cure her and after days of suffering, Mrs. Arana died and was buried in the village cemetery.

By the end of my second year, the new school was finished. No more dodging water dripping from the thatched roof or hopping over puddles. This was a two-room school built with cement foundation and it had a zinc roof. That cement smelled good, especially when it was wet. Every Friday afternoon, we had to wash the floor, a welcome relief from studying.

At home, Mama was still checking my notebooks everyday to see what I was being taught in school. She always made me read from the beginning of the literature book before I could read ahead. It didn't matter that the teacher hadn't gotten there yet. She did. After I was finished with my homework, I had to read the Bible out loud.

Mama completed Primary School and then spent her time on the farm with her parents. But the way she instilled the art of learning in me is unbelievable. When she taught me to read, I had to read 'sensibly.' The words had to be pronounced correctly, and I had to read with excitement.

Nothing was free. Parents found a way. Everyone I knew was poorer than the poorest American family, yet the family found a way to pay for textbooks, other school supplies, and uniforms; add tuition for a secondary education.

The textbooks were purchased from the Principal. When I received the year-end report card, it was accompanied with a booklist. I ran home, excited that I had passed, and showed my report card to Mama. Then I took it to Papa and told him how much money I needed for books. He put his hand in his pocket and brought out some money. After counting it, he handed it to me. I ran back to school and purchased my textbooks and workbooks for the next school year.

At the end of the six-week summer vacation, I had read all the books and learned how to spell all the new words. There was plenty of phonics in school but I was way ahead of what the teacher was teaching. I completed all activities in the workbooks. If there were things I didn't know, I left them alone until they were covered by the teacher. I studied very hard just so I could show off when school reopened after summer vacation.

The most important lesson Mama taught us was outside the text book: Read your Bible every day.

Follow the commandments. Do unto others as you would have them do unto you. Do the right thing. Forgive your enemies. If necessary, give the clothes off your back. Respect those in authority. She used to say, "Education, manners, and respect will carry you through the world."

"Children's children are a crown to the aged,

and parents are the pride of their children."

Prov. 17:6 NIV

**"I**f the children of today had to work like we did, they would strive for higher learning. We knew that the only way off the farm was to study, pass our exams, and graduate from high school. We did that, thanks to you, Mama. I always wanted to know why you pushed us so much to get an education, knowing that once we moved to the city, you and Papa would be left to work the farm. The little ones would not be of much help. Why didn't you just say, 'Okay, you are finished with primary school, join us on the farm?'"

"Gloria, I did not want you all to work as hard as I did. I didn't really know what was going to happen after you finished primary school, but I wanted my children to have a better education so you didn't have to do backbreaking work like I did. In the meantime, you had to work your way off the farm."

"Sister Vasquez's suggestion that I returned to primary school for another year was good for me. In addition, it gave me the opportunity to help the Principal who taught Standards 4, 5, and 6 (Grades 6, 7, and 8). When I got to school early, I peeked at her lesson plans and wrote the lessons on the board. At times, after direct instruction, she let me help Standards 4 and 5 with their lessons.

"I remember you coming home from a meeting with the Principal and telling Papa 'the Principal wants you to know she has no job for Gloria in the school so you had better send her on to college.' Those were the days when one or two students would finish primary school and then begin on-the-job training to become teachers right there in the school.

She believed that I was ready to leave for college. I was happy that she pushed you a little bit. I was the first female to leave that village for higher education and there were only about five boys who preceded me."

"Yes, and by the time your sister left two years later, more and more students were heading for the city."

"Some went to high school and others sought employment."

"I am proud of all my children."

"Mama, we are proud of you and I speak on behalf of all my brothers and sisters. You don't know how many times we commented that if it weren't for you, we would not be where we are today. You taught us to read and write before we went to school. Once we were in school, you lined us up every night and checked homework. We had to read and spell. We had to recite multiplication and division facts. We did not attend any birthday parties or any social events outside of school activities and even those were scarce.

"Remember the luncheon to celebrate the earning of our Master of Arts degree? Four of us accomplished that feat at the same time. During my speech I said, 'I hated my parents when I was growing up because I never had any fun. It was school, church, and plantation. While my classmates partied and traveled from place to place, I had to study and work. I couldn't understand it. Looking back, my parents did the right thing and that's why we can celebrate today.'"

"Aren't you glad?"

"Yes Ma'am. I always tell people that our family had the highest success rate, compared to other families."

"What does that mean?"

"If you put all the families of the village together and count how many of their children 'made it,' our family takes the prize. Seven out of eight went to college. The one who didn't, worked two jobs and retired from one. Those of us with degrees are still working."

"Always give thanks to God the Father for everything, in the name of our Lord Jesus Christ. Philippians 4:19 reads, 'But my God shall supply all your need according to his riches in glory by Christ Jesus.' And remember 'not of works, lest any man should boast.' You will find that in Ephesians 2:9."

"Amen. Mama, when it comes to quoting the scriptures, you are one of the few people that I trust. I don't have to verify…"

"I want you to read the scriptures for yourself."

"Yes Ma'am."

Mama began to hum and I joined in by saying the words and helping Mama with the singing:

> We thank thee each morning for a new born day
> Where we may work the fields of new long hay,
> We thank thee for the sunshine and the air that
> we breathed
> O Lord, we thank thee.
> We thank thee everyday as we kneel and pray

That we were born with eyes to see these things.

Thank thee for their love so pure and free

Oh Lord, we thank thee.

"For we will all stand before God's judgment seat.
So then each of us will give an account of
himself to God." Rom. 14:10b, 12 NIV

"Mama, somewhere, I have heard that you had a brother who went missing."

"That was my half-brother Joe. He lived in another village about fifteen miles north of where we lived with his mother, stepfather, and several step-brothers. In those days, people went to harvest Chiclets (chewing gum) in the jungle of Besileno. On their way, Joe and three of his half-brothers stopped by and spent the night with us. They mentioned that they would be gone for about four months.

"Early that morning, we got up, beat rice, cooked, and ate. Everyone seemed to be having a good time. Joe told Mum that when he returned, he was getting married. And they left.

"About a month after they left, the brothers sent word to their mother that Joe disappeared shortly after they had reached their destination."

"What did Pop do?"

"Pop and a few friends left to conduct their own search. They were gone six weeks but there were no signs of Joe."

"That must have been like looking for a needle in a haystack. How would they know where to look?"

"Well, there were lots of people who worked in the jungle. Pop talked to them and looked for bones or signs of a grave."

"I can't imagine how difficult that must have been, not only for Pop but for all of you."

"It was terrible."

"What about the law?"

"I was very young so I really don't remember much. The law back then was not like the law today. My family was suspicious of the brothers but we had no evidence of wrongdoing. As I grew up, I heard bits and pieces. Joe was not liked by his half-brothers. As the eldest, he was always chastising them for abusing their mother. Rumor had it that they murdered him. In fact, while drinking one night, they boasted about killing Joe. Two of them were involved in the murder and the third said nothing. They may have gotten away with a crime here on earth but they will have to answer for their transgression on judgment day."

Then as if the light went on in her head, Mama sang:

Across the bridge, there's no more sorrow.

Across the bridge, there's no more pain.

The sun will shine across the river

And you'll never be unhappy again.

Follow the footsteps of the King,

Till you hear the voices ring

They'll be singing out the glory of the land.

The river Jordan will be near

The sound of trumpets you will hear

And you'll behold the most precious place

ever known to man.

Mama stopped singing and recited the scriptures, "And be ye kind one to another, tenderhearted, forgiving one another, even as God for Christ's sake hath forgiven you."

"Do all things without murmurings and
disputings." Phil. 2:14 KJV

Members of Mama's family were always
around. When transportation by road from
the villages to the city became a reality, relatives
traveled from miles around and spent the night at our
house which was strategically located. In the mornings, the truck passed right in front of our house,
the last stop before reaching the ferry. As long as
someone was standing there, the driver stopped.

Our house was also an overnight stop for trav-
elers passing through from other villages. While
Mama eagerly offered a warm meal and a place to
rest, Papa was not that welcoming. Once they left,

Mama would be at the receiving end of his discontent. He was mostly upset that they came by with their 'empty hands' and he worked very hard to provide for his family. He would say, "You do not see me going around begging food and shelter."

Sometimes Mama said nothing; at other times, she responded, "They didn't beg for anything and it's not a crime to help those who are hungry, tired, or sleepy. Just remember that the happiest people on earth are the ones who have discovered the joy of giving."

Words like these sent Papa in a rage. He responded by uttering words that could not be printed while Mama conveniently grabbed her Bible and kept her eyes on the pages. She knew better than to argue with Papa. She never won an argument. Papa had the final word. Mama was smart. She knew how far to go to avoid physical consequences and she had her share.

Mama will not discuss their relationship, except to say, "But this one thing I do, forgetting those things which are behind, and reaching forth unto those things which are before. I press toward the mark for the prize of the high calling of God in Christ Jesus. I live by faith so I know I will eventually be rewarded by God."

Mama is singing again,

> When the roll is called up yonder,
> When the roll is called up yonder,
> When the roll is called up yonder
> I'll be there.

"Yes, you will, Mama."

"She gets up while it is still dark;

she provides food for her family..."

Prov. 31:15a NIV

"**M**ama, compared to other women in the village, you not only worked on the farm but you fished, too. Why didn't you stay home like all the other women?"

"I couldn't stay home. Your father said that if I didn't work, I wouldn't eat."

"Yes, but you worked more than he did."

"Gloria, I married your father for better or worse. My mother and father worked together and we had a good life. I wanted the same."

"You got up at three in the morning, left Papa in bed, and walked seven miles to fish. You were there early because that's when the fish were 'biting.' After cleaning the fish, you returned home by nightfall and cooked. Some of the fish was stewed; the rest fried so they could last a few days. When the food was ready, you served him. He ate and went to bed. You never complained. Why?"

"It wouldn't have done any good but started an argument. I was not only tired of the abuse but I was tired of eating white rice or boiled cakes so I went fishing. The Bible tells me to rejoice in my sufferings because suffering produces perseverance; perseverance, character; and character, hope and hope will not disappoint me because God has poured out love into my heart through the Holy Spirit."

"Mama, better you than me."

"What do you mean by that?"

"Nothing. I was just thinking out loud. Do you remember the time when that American man came and set up that cucumber farm? The farm was about

15 miles from home. You got up early and got us ready for school. Then you hitched a ride on a truck, and picked cucumbers all day in the hot sun to earn ten cents a bucket. One Friday, which was payday, Papa was very upset with you and threatened to beat you if you didn't give him some money. Did you give him the money?"

"I don't remember. Those days are gone. Why bring them up? The good Lord blessed me and gave me the strength to provide for you all. That's what I did."

"You had a way of providing. There were days when we had boiled cake for dinner every day (flour, salt, and baking powder mixed together and kneaded into small cakes which were boiled). We dipped it in cohune or coconut oil and ate it. I was tired of boiled cakes but in those days, children never complained. We ate what was placed in front of us. We had no choice. There was nothing else to eat. One Saturday, one of the hens laid an egg. You boiled that egg and cut it in four for the children. My quarter made the boiled cake taste better."

"The Bible says, 'I was young and now I am old; I have never seen the righteous forsaken or his children begging bread.' The Lord has always provided for us."

"Papa complained that he was tired of boiled cake. Sometimes you ignored him, but other times, you told him to bring what he wanted you to cook. That led to him cursing you. The words he used... I had never heard them anywhere before. You are a Christian. You never cursed back. Instead, you reminded him that he was showing a bad example to the children. That ticked him off even more and he threatened to beat you."

"Gloria, the Bible says 'Let your speech be always with grace.' I have forgiven and forgotten. Joseph forgave his brothers, didn't he? The Bible says, 'and we know that all things work together for good to them that love God, to them who are called according to His purpose.'"

"You are one of a kind, Mama."

"It was grace that taught my heart to fear and grace my fears relieved."

"When life hands you a lemon, make lemonade."

"Is that in the Bible?"

"No Ma'am. I heard it in one of Pastor Chappell's sermon." (Pastor Chappell is the senior pastor at Lancaster Baptist Church.)

"There is a hymn that we sang at Lancaster Baptist Church about God's grace. Do you remember it?"

I began to sing:

> Marvelous grace of our loving Lord,
> Grace that exceeds our sin and our guilt,
> Yonder on Calvary's mount outpoured,
> There where the blood of the Lamb was spilt.
> Grace, grace, God's grace,
> Grace that will pardon and cleanse within,
> Grace, grace, God's grace,
> Grace that is greater than all our sin!

"Thank you. That hymn lifts my spirit every time."

"I love it, too, Mama. It's one of my favorites."

"Cleanliness is next to godliness."
Harry Wesley, 1798

Ours was a two-storey house. Once we left upstairs in the morning, we did not go back up until dusk. It was important that the house always be in tip-top shape. Mama's famous words, "You don't know when there will be an emergency. You don't want people to come in here and find the place messy. They will talk bad about you after they leave." So we kept a clean house, kitchen, and yard. Mama is a stickler for cleanliness, even to this day.

Saturdays were work days especially during the school year. We were out of bed in the morning before the roosters crowed. Sleeping in? What's that? We

helped with the laundry (washing clothes by hand),
then moved to the kitchen and 'fixed tea' (breakfast).
After we ate, we washed the dishes, scrubbed the
fire hearth, and swept the kitchen. Usually, the floor
was divided into two sections. The section with the
dirt flooring was where all the cooking took place.
If sparks from the fire hearth or a piece of burning
wood fell on the floor, chances are there will be no
fire to burn the kitchen down. The eating section
was floored with board which we scrubbed with a
machete. A scrubbing brush would have done as
good a job, but that was too easy.

After cleaning the kitchen, we moved upstairs
with the machetes. The floors in the living room and
bedroom were made of mahogany, a scarce com-
modity in those days. Mahogany flooring was a good
indicator of cleanness or dirtiness. When it's clean,
it's red. If it's dirty, it looks black. That was how
Mama could tell when I missed a spot. Sometimes,
I was so tired that I wiped the floor with a wet cloth.
Then Mama came by and said, "Go back over it

again." I thought God gave her extra vision. It took me a while to figure out that the color of the wood betrayed me.

Now that the house and kitchen were cleaned, we moved to the yard. We chopped the bushes. Since we lived in the country, there were all different kinds of snakes slithering around. Papa was terrified of snakes and depended on his machete to kill them. While he chopped off their heads, Mama grabbed the nearest stick and beat them to death. This was a good reason to keep the yard clean - to see the slithering critters before they got too close to the house.

"Well Mama, you don't have to worry about getting blisters from machetes anymore."

Just when I thought Mama was out of scriptures to quote, she says, "Give thanks to God that we may live peaceful and quiet lives in all godliness and holiness."

"In the Book of Matthew, there is mention of the spirit returning and finding the house it left unoccupied swept clean, and put in order. Then he brought other spirits, more wicked than himself to live there. Houses shouldn't be that clean."

"Is that what the Bible says?"

"No Ma'am."

Mama gave me the 'look' and I pretended not to notice.

"And my God will meet all your needs
according to his glorious riches in Christ Jesus."
Phil. 4:19 NIV

D rinking water was a precious and scare com-
modity in my village. People who lived close
to the river had easy access to drinking water and had
gotten use to the non-filling, river-water taste. A few
villagers drilled a well in their backyard and were
lucky enough to find clean water. We had a well too,
but the water was undrinkable. The soil in our back
yard was mostly clay, so the water was either yellow
or it had a milky-white color. Sometimes it wasn't
even clean enough to do laundry.

We lived about a mile from the river but weren't allowed to go there (Papa's orders). Instead, we transported water from creeks at least a mile in the opposite direction. Melanie and I loaded two buckets on a stick then put the stick on our shoulder. She was in the front and I in the back. We carried water like this twice a day, every day, for nine years.

In the summer time, water was hard to find. We hopped out of bed around three in the morning and accompanied Papa and Mama to secret water holes that they had dug in the swamp the previous day. In the evenings after school, we raced up the road before the other children to retrieve water from the secret holes. When one ran dry, we moved to another. When all the holes ran dry, we waited for water to seep up. It took about an hour to fill a bucket.

During the rainy season, there was plenty of water which created another problem. The water was not clean since debris and mud from the swamps flooded and polluted the creeks. We had to search for clean water which was a skill we developed from an early age.

"Mama, do you remember the time I fell into the swamp. It was like a sinkhole. I had no idea that shrubbery and grass were growing on top of the mud. As far as the eye could see, it looked solid. I ventured out farther than normal and went down to my neck. Luckily, there were other children there waiting for water and pulled me out. You gave me a whipping when I got home. I don't know why."

"If you don't know, then I won't tell you."

Oops! It was time to change channel. "Now it's so easy to get water. Turn on the tap and out it comes."

"Don't forget that there are people in the world who still fetch and carry water for long distances. Some don't even have water to carry."

"Mama, I wonder if that's why it's not easy for people who live a difficult life to believe in someone they can't see. We tell them that Jesus loves them, yet they suffer. How can we quote scriptures to them about 'knock and the door will open, seek and ye shall find' and yet they experience hardships? How do we explain the river of the sanctuary referred to in Zechariah and Revelation when they do not have physical water?"

"Gloria, it is true that prayers are not immediately answered. The Bible reminds us to 'have faith in the Lord your God and you will be upheld; have faith in his prophets and you will be successful.' You have to believe first. Whether the water comes from a creek or a fountain, the Lord is the spring of living water."

"This is easy for the believer. How do you convince the non-believer? If the physical needs are not being met, how can the spiritual needs be addressed?"

"In Hebrews, Chapter 11, you can read about plenty of examples on faith. Read them. Share them. The Bible tells us that even if we are faithless, God will remain faithful. You have to believe first, then, take care of physical needs. You know Philippians 4:19. Tell it to me."

"And my God will meet all your needs according to His glorious riches in Christ Jesus."

"Do you believe that?"

"Yes Ma'am."

"God blessed them and said to them,
'Be fruitful and increase in number; fill the
earth and subdue it...'" Gen. 1:28 NIV

Back in the good old days, everything was so secretive when it came to having babies. Women stayed in their own homes and midwives delivered the babies. Midwives were usually the most elderly women of the village, probably over 60. They were assisted by a relative of the mother-to-be, usually the mother or a sister. For example, there was Grandma Goya, our neighbor. She wasn't our real grandmother but we called her Grandma. This was a sign of respect. She delivered babies not only in our village but in five other neighboring villages as well. When she couldn't make the journey by foot, someone brought a horse and escorted her to where she needed to be.

Children were never allowed in the house during delivery, unless it was night time. About the third day after the birth of the baby, the siblings got to peek under the net at, not hold, the new arrival. It would be a couple more weeks before we were allowed to hold the baby.

Mothers stayed in bed for nine days, most of the time under a net. The lucky ones had their mothers who came in and took care of household chores. Or, maybe there was a sister or sister-in-law nearby to help out. If not, for nine days, the midwife did the laundry for mother and baby. The rest of the family took care of their own laundry. There was no such luxury as disposable diapers; cloth diapers were the fad. Laundry was done by hand because there was no washer or dryer.

How many brothers and sisters do you have? There are eight of us. My cousins are too numerous to count. For example, Mama's eldest brother had fifteen children; her youngest, eight; Papa's youngest sister had twelve; one brother had ten. There were plenty of children in the homes. There was no such thing as birth control; neither was there a welfare system. Parents had children and took care of them. Parents found a way.

In 1955, I lost my first baby brother. I remember Mama had a big tummy. I heard her moaning during the night. The next morning, I heard Grandma Goya say, "You will have another son, Freddie," and she left. Then I saw Papa leave the room with a small carton box. I followed him down the stairs and into the back yard all the while maintaining a safe distance out of his sight. He walked about 200 yards from the kitchen, dug a hole, and placed the box into it. Nothing was said then or ever. I was in high school before I realized that the baby was 'stillborn.'

I was blessed with my second sister at the age of five. I went home for lunch and received the report from Grandma Goya. In my home, the midwife delivered the joyful news. "The stork brought you another sister," she said in her usual granny voice.

I went back to school and told my classmates that the stork brought me a baby sister. I can still hear Terence saying, "How can a bird bring you a baby sister when your mother had the big belly?"

"That's what Grandma Goya said." I had no reason to doubt her. We were trained to respect and believe our elders.

Terence laughed but I was saved by the bell. We lined up and walked into the classroom. As we prayed, I wondered if Terence was right. Mama did have a big belly. Maybe that's where the baby came from. But did the belly just burst open? That must have hurt.

Six of us were delivered by midwives. However, due to Mama's age, 40 and 45 respectively, the last two were born in the hospital. The only hospital was twenty-six miles away in the capital. Each time, the nurse sent Mama to the hospital where she rested for three months before giving birth. (If not, Papa would have worked her up to the time of delivery.) We never saw Mama during that time.

"Mama, back then, did you know about birth control?"

"No."

"You now know what it is, right?"

"Yes."

"Would you have used it if it was available?"

"No. What does the Bible say?"

"Increase and multiply, and parents should save up for their children. However, in this country, some women tend to have children just to collect money from the government. They have no education. No jobs. No parental skills. But they breed like rabbits, while those of us, who can afford children, have one or two, and pay for those who chose to have dozens. Is that fair? Look at the woman who had eight children at one time. She already had six, and was collecting State disability. A few years ago, I met the mother for one of my students. She was 33 years and had just delivered her eleventh child; this one by C-section. This woman never had a job in her life and was not supported by any of the nine men who fathered her children. The oldest was 13; the second one, Miguel, was driving his teachers crazy. In fact, he came to school as close to lunch time as possible, then after a free lunch, he slept in class."

"In Book of Genesis, the Lord says 'Be fruitful and increase in numbers.'"

"But it didn't say to pass on the burden of raising your children to someone else. What about taking responsibility for your actions? Mama, you missed one of Pastor Jay's sermons. It was entitled 'Faith in the Family.' He referred to the verse from 1 Timothy 5:8 (NIV) which reads 'If anyone does not provide for his relatives, and especially for his immediate family, he has denied the faith and is worse than an unbeliever.' I take this literally and figuratively. My point is if you can't afford them, don't have them."

"Gloria, let me tell you something. Children are a blessing from God." Then she commenced singing:

Jesus loves the little children,

All the children of the world.

Red and yellow, black and white

They are precious in His sight.

Jesus loves the little children of the world.

"If your enemy is hungry, give him food
to eat…" Prov. 25:21a NIV

We grew up being self-sufficient. What we didn't have, we went without, although it seemed as though we were the Salvation Army of the village. People were always begging for something. They never came when Papa was at home. It appeared as though they were peeking through the bushes and it was opened season when he left the premises.

"Ms. Middleton, can I borrow a pint of fat?" or "Ms. Middleton, my mama said if you can send her a pint of rice?"

I had a fit, outside the presence of Mama, of course. I let Melanie know how I felt. "Why couldn't they make their own fat or plant their own rice? While we labored all day, they were out partying. They never bring that stuff back." Moreover, Mama wouldn't take it back anyway.

We raised chickens and turkeys. The latter enjoyed trekking the two square miles around the village. When they didn't show up by nightfall, Melanie and I went house to house looking for them. We had to hustle, especially if it was a school night. We had homework to do.

A certain family lived less than a mile directly across from us. Their house was not visible from ours because of the dense thicket and shrubbery. Everyone, except Mama, knew that they were thieves. We heard it at school but did not dare repeat it at home.

One evening, two of the turkey roosters did not return home. Melanie and I set out looking for them. Usually, the villagers would say, "No, I didn't see them today," or "Look in the coop to see if they got mixed in with ours."

We left that certain family for the last as we circled around the village. This family consisted of a husband and wife, their teenage daughter and son; but the wife's boyfriend had moved in. As we approached the house, Ms. Nottingham, the wife, met us outside the door. I told her that we were looking for two of our missing roosters. She replied, "They didn't come here."

As Melanie and I walked home, we agreed that they stole the turkeys. How come she met us outside? She practically blocked our path from walking across their unfenced back yard.

We gave Mama the bad news. We were unable to find the turkeys.

About eight o'clock that evening, we were all upstairs doing homework. Papa nodded in his favorite chair. "Ms. Middleton?" Ms. Nottingham called from downstairs.

Mama walked out on the veranda, which ran the length of the house. "Good evening, Ms. Nottingham."

"I heard that you said that I stole your turkeys."

Mama was slow to answer, maybe shocked at the accusation. "I haven't left my house. I haven't spoken to anyone. Who told you that?"

Her boyfriend responded with more curse words that Lucifer. "...I told her so..."

Mama walked in the house and closed the door. Papa did not move.

Several weeks later, a motorcycle officer from the court arrived with a summons. Ms. Nottingham was suing Mama for accusing her of stealing the turkeys, even though Mama did not leave the house or talk to anyone. The officer was still at our house when we arrived home for dinner. He was introduced as Cousin Joe. I recounted what had occurred the night of the turkey search. Cousin Joe said, "Don't worry. Tell it to the Judge."

On the day of the trial, I was a witness. I was dressed up in my Sunday best. I got to miss school and go into the city, which was a luxury in those days. When I walked in the courtroom, the Judge asked, "How old are you?"

"Nine, Your Honor."

"Get that child out of my courtroom."

As I was escorted outside, I heard him say, "Case dismissed."

Not a week later, Ms. Nottingham's daughter was at our house borrowing flour and oil. Mama gave them to her.

"Melanie," I said, "can you believe that? They stole our turkeys, took us to court, and now come a-begging. Mama gave the stuff to her. What's wrong with Mama? I wish Papa were here. He would have driven that girl away."

Melanie said nothing.

This is Mama. If you ask for it, and she has it, you will get it. She never said "No." And to us, she always says, "Be generous and be willing to share."

"My house will be called a house of
prayer..." Matt: 21:13a NIV

In the old country, Mama woke up early and
read her King James Version of the Bible every
morning. Under the shaft of that kerosene lamp, she
read. She also sang plenty of hymns. She had her
own little service. In the afternoon, after she finished
her "work" she read the Bible and sang again. Mama
does the same thing today, except that the light bulb
has replaced the kerosene lamp.

Although Mama was not Catholic, she made sure
that her children participated in the Catholic tradi-
tions and activities. On Good Friday, our house was
Station Number 2 for Stations of the Cross.

On Sundays, once we arrived home from church, we ate, washed the dishes, swept the kitchen, and retreated underneath the house with our Bibles and hymnals.

"Mama, what do you think of the preachers now-a-days?"

"I just want them to preach the word of God. "

"I do, too, but I hate when the preachers exaggerate to convince the congregation to do or not do something."

"That's why you read the Bible so you can know if your pastor is preaching the word of God. If he isn't, then you find one who does."

"I have heard a few good preachers in my time, Mama, but others need to find a different profession."

"Pastor Jay, Pastor Chappell, and Pastor Pearson – those men preach the word of God."

Now I began to sing,

Precious memories how they linger
How they ever flood my soul.

In the stillness of the midnight
Precious sacred scenes unfold.

Precious father, loving mother
Precious memories of my childhood...

Mama whispered, "I wanted my family to grow in grace."

"We did, Mama."

Mama began to hum
    Amazing grace, how sweet the sound
    that saved a wretch like me.
    I once was lost, but now I'm found
    was blind but now I see.

"He will wipe every tear from their eyes.
There will be no more death or mourning or
crying or pain, for the old order of things has
passed away." Rev. 21:4 NIV

In the 1950s, there was only one hospital in the city and Pop (Mama's father) died there. I was six. I don't remember what we were doing in the city but I was at his house when they brought his body home in an ambulance. Two men carried a stretcher up the stairs and went into the bedroom. After they left, I peeked through the door and noticed that Pop was lying on the bed with a red handkerchief tied over his face. He was flat on his back with his hands by his side. This is the first time that I ever remember seeing Pop in person.

Then Cousin Mable, a lady with six fingers on each hand, went into the room and started screaming, "Uncle! Uncle!" Mama pulled me away from the door. When I was younger, it was difficult to know who the real relatives were. Everyone was an auntie, uncle, cousin, grandpa, or grandma.

Later that day, a man I did not know, entered the room. When he left, I sneaked up to the door and peeked in again. Pop was all dressed up. He was in a white suit, the red handkerchief was removed from his face, and his silver-colored hair was nicely comb. Pop was very light-skinned. He could have passed for Caucasian. Then I felt Mama's hand on my backside. Two men needed the space to carry a big box (coffin) into the room. This time I stayed where she plopped me until I was told to move.

The house was about 500 yards from the banks of the Reggae River. At sunset, we all walked down to the river and climbed into a boat. The coffin was laid under the two rows of seats. I remember, trying to stretch my feet down to touch the coffin. A lady, who I didn't know, gave me the 'look' and the stretching stopped.

We traveled up the river all night and arrived on Pop's ranch early the next morning. There were lots of people at the house. Later that afternoon, the little children were left in the house while the adults walked about three hundred yards away to bury Pop right there on his ranch. Back then, most people were buried on their property. Mum cried for days but most of her children were there to comfort her. Except for Mama, all Mum's children lived within a two-mile radius.

Mum had buried two of her daughters before I was born. The eldest, Mrs. Santos, died and left a husband and four boys. The other daughter, Louise, died before her twentieth birthday. Because of the bits and pieces of information in my head, I recently asked Mama about Louise. Mama recalled that Louise was always in terrible pain. There were times when fluid was leaking from her breasts. She went to the only doctor in the city, maybe the country, but he was unable to diagnose the problem. So the family resorted to what was referred to as "bush medicine" but that did not help Louise. In those days, especially in the villages, people depended on local herbs and plants for healing. Different concoctions were handed down from generation to generation. To this day, some people still depend on them.

"Mama, you lost both parents and two sisters before you were 40. Do you remember how you felt? Were you angry at anyone?"

"Gloria, my parents lived by the good Book and that's how we were raised to 'grow in grace, and in the knowledge of our Lord and Savior Jesus Christ. To Him be glory both now and forever.' Keep in mind that this world is not our home. We are only passing through. It's always sad to lose your loved ones. Remember when Jesus comforted His apostles? The Bible tells us that Jesus reassured them that He was going to His father's house to prepare a place for them and that He would return and take them to be with Him. There is no need to be angry with anyone. We were always taught to be ready."

"I wonder about death. Why do we have to die? Why not just take us up to Heaven?"

"Death comes to all men because we all have sinned, and the wages of sin is death. No one will escape death. Pop, Mum, Louise, Mrs. Santos, and Mrs. Perez went home to be with the Lord and they are waiting for me. We will all meet again on that beautiful shore." And she sang,

> There's a land that is fairer than day,
> And by faith we can see it afar,
> For the Father waits over the way
> To prepare us a dwelling place there.
>
> In the sweet by and by,
> We shall meet on that beautiful shore;
> In the sweet by and by,
> We shall meet on that beautiful shore."

"Show proper respect to everyone."

1 Peter 2:17a NIV

When I was growing up, respect was a word not taken lightly. Women who were married always heard 'Mrs.' before their married surname.

Mama respects everyone. She always refers to her sisters as Mrs. Santos, Mrs. Perez, and Mrs. Harper; to her brothers as Brother or My Brother. Her sisters call her My Sister or Mrs. Middleton; she was Ma Dell or My Sister to her brothers.

Even married women younger than Mama receives her respect. She always precedes their last name with Mrs. If she doesn't know the married surname, she says Mrs. Henry (first name of the husband). Men are always Mister. She trained us the same way.

Four months after my daughter Elsie got married, she visited Mama. Even though Mama could not remember her married name she still used the word Mrs. She called her Mrs. Matt, the first name of her husband. Elsie said, "Grandma, you can still call me Elsie."

You can guess Mama's response. "No Ma'am. I was raised to call a married woman Mrs."

I said, "But Mama, she is your grandchild. You raised her."

"It does not matter. She gets the respect to which she is entitled."

"Sing and make music in your heart to the
Lord..." Eph. 5:19b NIV

In addition to reading the Bible every day, we also sang hymns. We learned to read at an early age, not only because Mama taught us from 'reading books' but by reading the Bible and singing from the hymnals.

Mama's youngest sister, Aunt Vicky, also moved to Langley with her husband. She lived a mile from our house, so we saw her often. Mama and Auntie were very close. When one has, both have. For example, when Auntie or her husband went fishing, Mama received her share. When we slaughtered a cow, Auntie was called to assist and take what she wanted. When one cooked a special dish, the other got her share.

When Auntie was in the 'motherly way', I went over and helped with the cooking and washing. I was between the ages of 11 and 13. While I worked, Auntie read the Bible and sang hymns. When I heard a hymn that I did not know, she taught it to me. That's where I learned plenty of hymns. Our hymns in the Catholic Church were good but not 'down home' like those.

Mama and Auntie's love of God and their praise of Him began in their parents' home. It's a practice they continued and taught their children.

One summer, Auntie came to America for a brief vacation. That's the happiest I have seen Mama in years. Auntie and Mama spent a few months with one of my sisters, who later reported that Mama and Auntie praised God every day. She left them reading the Bible in the mornings and when she returned home in the evenings, they were singing hymns of praise. She heard their melodic voices as soon as she exited her car, about two hundred yards away. I was not surprised. They did the same thing at my house. I just joined them.

Mama was never afraid or embarrassed to speak about God. In 2002, I changed jobs and bought a house about an hour's drive from where we were living. I took Mama to see the house. The sellers were still living there. As the husband gave us a tour, Mama asked, "Is there a good church around here?"

"Oh, yes, there's plenty. "

"But do they preach the word of God?" Mama had to know.

"There is a big church on the other side of town."

"Is it far from here?"

"About twenty minutes."

"Is there where you go?" I could tell the man was getting uncomfortable.

"No. We went there a few times. It's really big, but it seems like they don't let outsiders in. It seems to be made up of family and friends."

"Where do you go now?"

"We don't…"

It was time for me to interrupt. "Mama, please leave the man alone. Sir, can you please give me the name of the big church? I will check it out."

After we moved, we visited the church. It was Lancaster Baptist Church. We loved it. Aunt Vicky did, too. From time to time, Mama reminded me that, "Pastor Chappell can preach, the music isn't noisy, and I know some of the hymns."

Aunt Vicky went home to be with the Lord in 2005, and we always joke about her singing with the angels morning, noon, and night.

Sometimes, when it is quiet, I can hear Mama and Auntie's angelic voices singing: On a hill far away…, Jesus keep me near the cross…, It is well with my soul…, Because he lives, I can face tomorrow… What a fellowship, what a joy divine… and others. No choir was needed when they got together. I can't even imagine what Heaven will be like with the two of them there; no, make that six: Pop, Mum, Louise, Mrs. Santos, Aunt Vicky, and Mama.

"But if a widow has children or grandchildren, these should learn first of all to put their religion into practice by caring for their own family and so repaying parents and grandparents, for this is pleasing to God." 1Ti. 5:4 NIV

By 1961, I had four sisters. Mama was gone a lot. She accompanied Mum all over the country to get medical help, but not from physicians. They couldn't cure Mum's illness. Based on referral from friends, they went searching for a 'bush doctor', a person who provided treatment using a concoction of various herbs and plants. Mum was looking for treatment for what we now believed was cancer.

Children were children and were treated as such. We were never privileged to important information. Mama was gone for weeks at a time and I couldn't understand why she wouldn't take us along.

I did not like being with Papa. He was stricter than Mama and frankly, I was afraid of him. I saw how he treated Mama. Nothing was good enough for him. He found fault with everything. He whipped us with the rope he used to catch the horses. I was on pins and needles when Mama wasn't there.

I grew up very quickly. I learned how to cook and do laundry from about the age of seven. Papa helped with the cooking on school days but the kitchen had to be cleaned before he entered it. After he cooked, everything was such a mess, we had to clean it up and wash everything before we could eat. Nevertheless, everyone pitched in. No one complained. Mama was not there, and Papa was in charge. When he was out of sight, I was next in command.

The only close relative was Aunt Vicky who lived about a mile away, but Papa did not want help from her or anyone else. Even when people cooked and sent us food, he threw it away. When Auntie stopped by and offered assistance, he told her that everything was under control.

One day, soon after Mama returned from a trip with Mum, Uncle Danny, her youngest brother brought news that Mum was very sick. Mama got ready and left.

The next day, Uncle returned. Mum had passed away. Papa saddled two horses and we made it to Mum's ranch before nightfall. The ten-mile journey took about three hours. People filed in from neighboring villages. All the grandchildren retreated to the kitchen for tea (supper), while the adults were busy. Women cooked; some of the men built the coffin; others prepared the gravesite.

I enjoyed the wake. People sang without the accompaniment of hymnals and musical instruments, as one person recited the lyrics. They ate and sang all night. When daylight broke, most of the people headed home. It rained all day. By nightfall, most of the same people had returned. They helped in every way they could, from babysitting to cooking.

The funeral was scheduled for the following day and it was raining. People were commenting about what a great person Mum was and that the rain was a sign that her soul was in Heaven. She was dressed in white and laid in the coffin. She looked so beautiful. The coffin was placed on a stand built under the house for the occasion. Around ten in the morning, someone mentioned that the 'body was swelling up.' Right after that, people walked out in the rain to bury Mum beside Pop.

We returned to Langley the day after the funeral. Once I walked into our house, it finally dawned on me that I would never see Mum again. She was gone. She would never witness the birth of another grandchild. For the first time since her death, I cried silently. There was no time to grieve at Mum's place. There were so many people, and children were isolated from all the grief.

Years later, Mama shared more about the day Mum died. When Mama and Uncle Danny arrived at Mum's house, it was raining. Of course, mud was transferred from Mama's shoes to the steps. As sick as she was, Mum got up, took a bucket with water, and washed the stairs.

Later that evening, while in bed, Mum was served fried fish for tea. After she ate, someone brought a wash cloth but she insisted on getting up and washing her hands and mouth. On her deathbed, she was surrounded by her three surviving daughters and four sons. They read the Bible and sang hymns. After a while, Mum looked out the window. It was dark outside. "Pop is calling me," she said. "Can you see him? He is outside next to that tree. He is waiting for me." Then she closed her eyes and died.

Every time I think about Mum, I always remember the night she died. Did Mum really see Pop? From all accounts, she was not hallucinating. Is that what love is all about? Pop must be in Heaven because if he were in Hell, Mum would not have seen him.

They are both in Heaven now. I heard that's where the good people reside.

When I see other children with their grandparents, it brings back memories of Mum. Even though I knew her for a short period of time, she was loving and kind. Regardless of the event, she made things fun. When she came for the birth of my third sister, a bat had gotten under our net. Once Mum released it from under the net, she chased it around the house with a pair of scissors. She had us laughing as she lounged after it and deliberately missing it. When it was finally caught, Mum released it outside in the moonlight.

That was the last time she visited us. Sometime after that visit, she became ill and for the next two years, she and Mama traveled around the country to find a cure for her illness.

Mama raised both of my daughters while I worked. For that, I am extremely grateful. She taught them to read and write and recite their multiplication facts before they started school. She taught them how to sing, pray, and read their bible every day. Most of all, she taught them how to live a Godly life.

Now Mama is relaxing. All her children are successful, and she takes turns spending time with each of them, still preaching from the Bible and making sure that they are raising her grandchildren in a God-fearing home.

It takes a village to raise a child.

Yes, it takes a village to raise a child. This is so true.

I was raised during the time when your biological parents were in the home, but your unofficial adopted parents were the villagers. Parents raised their children. Everyone believed that 'manners and respect will carry you through the world.' I heard those words every single day.

In school, children respected the teachers and each other. No rules or consequences were posted. You learned them at home. Teachers had the authority to discipline children. If you were one of the unfortunate few, you hope that word didn't reach your par-

ents. If it did, be ready for whipping Number Two.
I have *NEVER* heard any student talking back to a
teacher, much less yelling at or cursing at them, like
they do here in America. Any student who appeared
to have an 'attitude' did not have any friends. No one
wanted to be around troublemakers.

Teachers did more than teach. They were guardian
angels. They had the interest of students and parents
in mind. Here is a good example: No one had money
to 'waste'. Every shilling was precious. Once I found
a shilling. Well, I found the place in the ceiling where
Mama stashed the handkerchief with her shillings. I
removed one (twenty-five cents), took it to the gen-
eral store, bought chewing gum and candy, took them
to school, and shared them with my classmates.

The store owner was concerned. He asked me
where I got the money. I told him that Mama gave
it to me. He replied, "I should keep this money until
I see her. I know your mother wouldn't give you
money to spend on candy."

I should have put the money away; instead, I had a good answer. "She gave it to me for being Number One in the class." He had no reason to doubt me. Everyone in the village knew that I was smart. There was no phone in those days. What a difference a telephone would have made!

Teachers are nosey but in a good way. Miss Baptist saw me distributing gum and candy. She confiscated what she could from my classmates and me, and followed me home for dinner (lunch in America). In those days, everyone went home for dinner unless you lived three miles away. Then you go home with a classmate, or ate your Journey cake, bread, tortilla, or flap jack at school.

Money did not grow on trees. Before Miss Baptist was finished with her report, Mama went over to a patch of berry trees, tore off the biggest branch that she found, threw me on the ground, held up one of my legs, and beat the daylights out of me. She beat me until I couldn't scream anymore. It seemed like she was flogging me forever. When she stopped, I could barely walk. Miss Baptist witnessed it all.

It was not the end of the school day. I returned to school with welts all over my body. Everyone knew what had happened. I couldn't even talk because I was so hoarse from screaming. I was embarrassed. Not one student said a word.

Tough love! Pastor Jay presented a series entitled "Catch the Vision for Tough Love." Had he been my Pastor at the time, he would have referred me to Hebrews 12:11 (NIV) which reads, 'No discipline seems pleasant at the time, but painful. Later on, it produces a harvest of righteousness and peace for those who have been trained by it.'

Mama never spared the rod. If her children misbehaved, regardless of where they were, the board of education was applied to the seat of administration. My siblings recounted an incident at school that required immediate attention. The Principal sent for Mama and Aunt Vicky. Apparently, cousins from both families were involved in a dispute with members of another family. Mama was not interested in hearing whose fault it was. Once she got there, she beat her children and Auntie did the same, right there at school, in front of everyone. If the Principal did not intervene, even the innocent would have been whipped.

The whole village was like one large extended family. Everyone knew everyone because families remained in the village for generations. Students moved together through the Standards, unless retention stood in the way. Each student had to successfully master the requirements for each Standard before moving on to the next. Social promotion was not an option. There was no such grade as a D. Seventy percent was passing. Anything less that seventy percent and you repeated the Standard.

Students didn't change schools like they do in America. We studied together. We played together. We prayed together. More time was spent competing to be Number 1 that there wasn't enough energy left for fighting and bickering. Families supported the teachers and activities at school. As students and children, we aimed to please. Everyone wanted his or her family to be known as the smartest and most respectful.

On the way home from school, the eyes of the villagers were on you. You had better be on your best behavior, or you would not make it home in one piece.

Children feared adults, but this was a good thing. Most of the time, adults didn't have to say much, just that look! According to Mama, the villagers had unwritten permission to discipline us. By the way, you never heard children say, "You are not my mama, so you can't tell me what to do."

How I long for those days.

"I rejoiced with those who said to me,

'Let us go to the house of the Lord.'"

Ps. 122:1 NIV

Vatican II instituted a most welcome change. Catholics could now participate in non-Catholic services, without fear of being ex-communicated.

In 1963, a Baptist minister arrived in the village. He was interested in building a church which would be staffed by a missionary couple from Oregon. A house had to be built, and a pastor from the city would visit one Sunday a month. Voluntary support from the community was essential.

Mama worked every day, mixing cement and doing whatever she could to help build the church.

Other villagers helped even though they were Catholics. Within a few months, the small Baptist Church was completed with seating for about 75 people. By the end of the year, the two-storey house with a kitchen was built.

Mr. and Mrs. Bennett were in their late sixties or early seventies and the nicest White folks we had ever met. Whatever Mama cooked or baked, she sent their portion. Pretty soon, Mrs. Bennett taught Mama to prepare certain foods the American way and Mama taught her how to cook local dishes. Mama was their guide as the couple traveled from village to village spreading God's Word.

My sisters and I followed Mama every Saturday evening to prepare the church for services the next day. We washed and swept the floor, dusted the benches, and cleaned the church yard.

Services were scheduled for 11 A.M., the same time Mass ended for Catholics. The Baptist Church was only a stone's throw away, so after Mass, my siblings and I headed there to meet Mama.

I am proud of Mama. She was by our side through all the Catholic regalia, but *her* church was opened when we were old enough to attend Mass by ourselves. She got us ready and sent us on our way. She never told us to show up at her church. We did because we enjoyed the singing and the togetherness which a small group provided. Mrs. Bennett played the piano and led the singing while Mr. Bennett conducted the services. I felt as though I was in the house of God.

Even after Mama came to America, she put in her time cleaning the churches she attended. Once I really upset her. You could count the Black families in this church on one hand; in fact, there were two. Once a month, Mama went to the church to help with the cleaning. I found out that she was always on her knees cleaning the floor. So I said to her, "You are not a slave. That's not your job. Let someone else take a turn on the floor for a change."

She said, "Gloria, it doesn't bother me. I do what I can to prepare the house of the Lord."

When we moved to Sunrise Church, Mama donated her time in the nursery. She served the children for over twelve years. One Christmas I dared to ask, "Has anyone ever given you a gift or thank you card?"

"For what? I don't need a thank you card. This is my church and I am willing to help in any way I can. Everyone should do the same."

"...for death is the destiny of every man;

the living should take this to heart."

Eccles. 7:2 NIV

I never met my paternal grandfather. He died in 1951 after a long illness. I never knew him but met his wife, my grandmother, in 1963.

Going to the city was a luxury. I was in the city for my first entrance examination. If I passed, I would be able to go to high school. The day before the exam, Papa took me over to my aunt's house to meet their mother.

Grandma was blind and lived with her youngest daughter. I only saw her for a few minutes. She was sitting in a chair in the living room. Her long silver-colored hair extended down to her waist. She was petite and light-skinned and reminded me of a Mayan woman. She didn't say much, but sometime after that meeting, I learned that she lived with Mama and Papa until I was about two, then she moved with her youngest daughter to help raise her children.

When I went to school, it was customary to go home at noon for dinner. This was not an issue because everyone lived in walking distance, usually within two square miles of the school. Students from neighboring villages brought their dinner or went home with their classmates.

It was during one of these dinner breaks that bad news arrived. Just months after I had met Grandma, one of the neighbors heard on the radio that Papa's mother had died. Papa was eating and I noticed a few tears rolled down his cheeks. That was the only time I ever saw tears from him.

The radio was our means of communication. At that time, there was only one station, Radio Besileno. For a small fee, they would read the message. Before announcing a death, they played what I referred to as the "Death Tune." Life stopped when that tune played. Everyone listened and hoped that it wasn't a family member or an acquaintance leaving for a better place.

By the time I was 13, both sets of grandparents had died. They all suffered before dying. For sure, I know that my maternal grandparents are in Heaven.

"What time I am afraid, I will trust in thee."

Ps. 56:3 NIV

For whatever reason, Papa did not go to church. I never heard him pray nor have I seen him with the Bible. Maybe, that's why he was always afraid, of something.

Recently, Mama mentioned that Papa was afraid of going to the hospital. "Once, your father was sick. I told him that I would take him to the hospital. He cried and said, 'You just want to get rid of me. You want me to die.' So I left him alone."

Looking back, my dad was afraid of the dead and maybe even of dying. Again, there wasn't much conversation in our house. Regardless of who died, Papa never went to the funeral. I was there when one of his favorite nephews died. He was at the home prior to the funeral procession, but I never saw him after that.

Earlier I mentioned that the kitchen was built away from the house. Once, our kitchen was about two hundred yards from the house. There were times when Papa traveled between both buildings early in the morning, and I would hear a barrage of curse words. As a child that was scary. Once in a while, he explained the incident to Mama. He mentioned that he always saw a woman with long hair. The only way to make her disappear was to curse her.

It was suggested that the house may have been built on a burial plot. But as far as we know, no one had lived on that property for centuries. Based on what I have learned, it could only have been the Mayas. However, there could be another reason. According to rumors, Papa was born with "call", a type of veil over his face and that was why he saw ghosts. Whatever the reason, he would never be caught outside after dark or at anyone's wake or funeral.

Mama was always saying to him, "Go and read your Bible. If you believe in God, you wouldn't have to fear the devil. The Lord says, 'Do not fear for I am with you.'"

Papa would respond negatively, and although Mama knew she would lose, she recited a few more Biblical verses, like 'trust in God and He will save you', then she kept quiet.

"...if any would not work, neither should
he eat." 2 Thess. 3:10 KJV

As I grew older, more siblings were added to
the family. Things didn't change much in
our house. School convened on Saturdays, and every
night Mama lined us up for reading, spelling, and
recitation of multiplication facts.

We were also spending more time on the plantation, especially if it was on the fifty acres behind our
house. Here is a typical day during planting of the
crops. We got up at 4 A.M. and put on 'plantation
clothes.' Then we walked about half an hour to the
plantation. While Papa and Mama made holes in the
ground with a stick, Melanie and I walked behind

and dropped rice or corn seeds in them. Most of the time, Mama helped with the planting. In the meantime, the two or three younger siblings were left at home in bed.

By 7 A.M. we were on our way back home. We fed chickens, swept floors, washed dishes, carried water from the well for the laundry, walked one mile up the road and fetched drinking and cooking water from a creek, bathed, and got ready for school. When the school bell rang at 9 A.M., we were always standing in line. Being late was not an option, so we hustled and completed our chores.

School was out at 3:30 P.M. We ran home. Just so we wouldn't hang around with our friends, Papa spat on the ground (at least that's what he told us). If it dried before we got home, a whipping was promised. School was less than a mile away so we ran home, then changed into our 'plantation clothes.' This had to be done in seconds because Papa was on his way down the road to the plantation.

We were scared to walk by ourselves. Stories were told of 'little men' who carried children away. We made sure that we were right on Papa's heel. We had no idea those stories were made up to scare us straight. Mama was more patient. She gave us more time to change and that upset Papa.

We worked on the plantation until sunset. Then we returned home, fed and locked up the chickens and turkeys, helped in the kitchen: made tea (supper), washed dishes, swept floors, then moved upstairs. This was our routine during planting, weeding, or harvesting time.

Earlier in my youth, schools across the country received a break for six weeks, beginning in May and ending mid-June. This was for the students to help their parents on the farm. This changed to July when I was in Standard IV (grade 6) so children could help with the harvesting of crops.

We had to help our parents. We were the unpaid, hired helpers. Mama worked every day by Papa's side. No family had money to buy the groceries needed to feed all the children. Women had as many children as they could, so farming really helped. Farmers planted as many crops as would grow.

Don't even consider getting sick. My mother worked whether she was one month or eight months pregnant. Papa made it quite clear, "If you do not work, you will not eat."

It was night time but our day was not finished yet. All of the children sat around this big table and cowered under the kerosene lamp. After we were finished with homework, Mama lined us up every school night and we had to read, spell, and recite multiplication facts. We had to know everything. If we were called upon twice and did not show prog-ress, we were locked outside the door.

Was this a bad thing? Picture living out in the country. The closest house on each side of you was about 600 yards away. It was very dark. Even if it was a full moon, you saw shadows. Imagine being raised knowing that there were 'little men' outside who would carry you away for not knowing how to spell all your words or recite multiplication facts.

There were a few times when I was locked outside. I did not bang on the door but I stayed on the top step and screamed. Most of the time, I was rescued. When Grandma Goya, our adopted grandma got tired of the screaming, she came in hearing distance and yelled, "I beg for her. She will study her lesson."

Of course, Mama respected her elder and would open the door with these words, "You better know it this time, or else no amount of begging will help you."

Notice, there was no consideration for being up early, for putting in a day's worth of work at school and on the plantation, and doing chores. We were expected to study and remember everything. But that's how it was. There were no complaints, either.

Mama used to tell us, "If you don't want to do back-breaking work for the rest of your life, get an education." That was enough of an incentive for us but in the meantime, we had to do backbreaking work. During summer vacation, we 'cut' rice and 'broke' corn. I enjoyed this time, because once the corn was removed from the husk and boiled, I ate as many as three at one sitting. "Sweat" rice was tasty. This is fresh-cut rice steamed in the shell, then dried, beaten, and cooked. It was delicious.

Never a day went by that Mama wasn't reading to us or having us read to her. Even when our eyes weren't in school books, they were in the Bible.

Mama and Aunt Vicky were the only two women in the village who spent time with their husband on the plantation. Maybe, it was because my father expected boys and ended up with five girls in a row. Maybe, Mama and Auntie took the Bible literally and obeyed their husband. Whatever the reason, we worked. Papa used to say, "If you do not work, you will not eat." That applied to everyone.

Mama did not go beyond primary school. Yet, she did everything to get us educated. She realized that although 'hard work does not kill anyone' she wanted us to have it easier than she did. We worked on the farm until we graduated from high school.

When I was in high school, I bought my books for the next school year and took them home during the summer. To get out of going to the plantation, I told Mama that I had homework. Papa didn't buy it but Mama gave me a break most of the time. If I didn't go to the plantation, I had to do housework: wash, cook, clean. There were times when I felt guilty and helped out on the plantation.

~~⊗~~

..."I was sick and you looked after me..."

Matt. 25:36 NIV

M ama would help Papa cut the plantation (fell trees and cut shrubbery with axe and machete). After the plantation was burned, the children helped with the planting of crops. Then Papa went North, about seventy miles away, to plant watermelons, bananas, and plantains. Mama was left behind to weed the plantation. I helped. From an early age, I learned to use the machete.

One Saturday morning, Mama took Melanie and me to the plantation to remove the weeds from the rice and corn. I was ten and Melanie eight. The other three children were left at home. One was five, another three, the third less than one year. Food was left on the table and my siblings knew what to do. Back then it was safe to leave your children at home. Mama had hoped to be home by eleven. We weeded non-stop for about four hours. It was about 85 degrees F and getting hotter by the minute. Mama looked up at the sun and announced that it was time to stop. Melanie and I moved under the hut, a thatched roof on four posts.

As Mama walked toward the hut, she noticed a small patch that needed weeding and went over to weed it. I picked up my machete and went to help her. (Even as a young child, I felt sorry for Mama – the way she had to work, or else...). No sooner had I started, than the machete slipped off a root and landed on the big toe of my left foot. I saw blood and screamed. Mama dropped her machete, picked me up and carried me under the hut. She told me to sit still. Then she picked up some burnt ashes and put them on the wound. After a few minutes, the flow of blood was down to a trickle.

"Melanie, watch your sister until I get back." Mama went to look for a horse. She had no rope.

Luckily, the horses were familiar with her. She brought one back by the mane, put me on it, and led us home. When we got home, she washed off the ashes, dressed and bandaged the wound, and put me to bed.

Days later when the bandaged was removed, I realized the severity of my injury. I almost cut off my big toe. Only a piece of skin kept it in place. Mama dressed that wound every day until it healed. Almost five decades later, the scar is still there reminding me from whence I came and a Mother's love that cannot be equaled.

Mama looked after the villagers with the same fervor as she did her family. As word trickled out that someone was sick, Mama was there providing whatever assistance she could. If the woman of the house was sick, and the family was poorer than us, Mama sent food daily. She visited regularly if only to read the Bible and sing hymns. This was a tradition she continued even in America. She always looked out for those in need.

"…a wife must not separate from her
husband." 1 Cor. 7:10 NIV

'What God has joined together, let no man put asunder.' When I was growing up, I heard these words from Mama but had no clue what she was talking about. Now, I know. Mama takes these words literally. There is no reason for a divorce. You cannot give her a good reason. She believed that a couple should do everything to stay married, whether or not they have children.

I remember how distraught she was, when, after six years of marriage, the wife of a dear friend had filed for divorce. Mama said, "This makes no sense. Have you heard her excuses for a divorce?"

"No Ma'am. What did she say?"

"She told the Pastor, 'My husband loves the kids more than me. He wasn't there when my first child was born, and we never had a honeymoon.'"

"Mama, those are the dumbest reasons I have ever heard. I bet she found another man on the job."

"I told the young man to talk to his mother-in-law. I can't believe she will allow such thing."

I tried to convince Mama that the girl's Mother was in on it. But Mama said, "Gloria, I would not encourage you to leave your husband for those, those... those aren't good reasons. He needs to talk to her mother."

"Mama, talking to his mother-in-law won't do any good. I don't have to remind you that both women divorced their first husbands."

"The Bible says, 'What God has joined together, let no man put asunder.' That young man is suffering right now. He believed that his marriage was going to last forever."

"This is a new day and time, Mama. Until death do us part does not mean the same as it did when you took your vows. Life is filled with trials and temptations but you cannot be sad or despondent. You told us to rejoice that we are participating in the sufferings of Christ and we will be overjoyed when His glory is revealed. The young man is a believer and he will get through this adversity. If you have faith to believe, ask of God and receive."

Mama closed her eyes and softly sang,

> He leadeth me, O blessed thought,
> O words with heavenly comfort fraught.
> What e'er I do, Where e'er I be,
> Still 'tis God's hand that leadeth me.

~~~~~~

So they are no longer two, but one.

Therefore what God has joined together, let

man not separate." Matt. 19:6 NIV


I f anyone *ever* had just cause to walk away from her husband, Mama did. In a church before God and man, she uttered the words, "Until death do us part." That was a promise she intended to keep "come hell or high water."

Looking back, Mama was literally afraid of her husband. Most of the time, she did nothing to defend herself and at times, when she did speak up, there were consequences, both physical and mental. By the time I was thirteen, I have had enough.

It was New Year's Day, about noon. The family was seated around the dinner table. Papa mentioned that he was going into the city the next day. At the time, he was in hog heaven. He had his first son (after five girls). My brother was two. Papa said to him, "Boy, while I am gone, you are in charge. When I come back, I want you to tell me everything that happened when I was away. You give the orders and everyone must listen to you. If they don't, you can beat them."

I looked at my brother and said, "Don't even think about it. You hit me with a piece of iron and I didn't tell on you. You will not get away with it again."

Mama said, "Freddie, train Junior to have manners and respect. He is a child. He cannot beat anyone in here. That's not the way to bring up a child..."

Wham! Papa slapped her right across the face and walked out of the kitchen. As the tears flowed down Mama's cheeks, Melanie and I cried softly as tears flowed down our cheeks, too.

Later that day, I joined Mama upstairs. I remembered reading about a wife who left her husband. The story didn't say anything about her going to Hell. I knew what I read in the Bible 'until death do us part.' But someone broke those vows so what's the big deal. This was the first time I had ever gotten involved. Beside what we had witnessed, neither parent had ever said anything bad about the other to us. There was never any type of discussion about life - nothing. As children, we knew our place. But I had to take a chance. "Mama, why do you stay with him?"

"Only because of you, my children. Now, go and read your Bible."

As I walked away, I heard Mama reciting Psalm 23: the Lord is my Shepherd; I shall not want. He maketh me to lie down in green pastures; He leadeth me beside the still waters...

I joined Melanie under the house. "If he touches her again, I will get the machete and chop off his head when he is asleep."

Mama stayed married for fifty-three years. Death separated them in 2003 when Papa left to meet his Maker. Mama had nothing negative to say. From time to time, I try to bring up an incident that I remember, but she has no recollection about it. I get the message.

"Do not seek revenge or bear a grudge against one of your people, but love your neighbor as yourself. I am the Lord." Lev. 19:18 NIV

Coming to America, presented a whole new challenge for me. I had to deal with racial prejudice; however, I never let the color of my skin slowed me down. I aimed to please. I worked very hard. Consequently, more doors were opened to me compared to some African-Americans.

I left the Army in 1976 and worked as a Correctional Officer for the local Sheriff's Department. Months later, the department announced that it was hiring its first females for patrol duty. I applied but two white women were hired instead.

We all went to the Sheriff's Academy at the same time and I whipped both of them academically and physically. Nevertheless, I was not promoted to patrol.

The seventies was a time for Affirmative Action. Remember that? Employers were required to hire a certain number of minorities.

Just before graduating from the Academy, representatives from several police agencies came to the Academy and the Administrator invited me to interview with them. He promised that the interviews would be kept confidential, since I was employed with the Sheriff's Department which was paying for my training. Prior to enlisting in the Army, I was a police woman in my native Besileno and wanted to return to the streets.

During the interviews, I made it quite clear to all the panelists that I did not want to be hired to fulfill the requirements of Affirmative Action. I wanted to be hired because I was qualified for the job. Moreover, whoever hired me would be getting three employees for the price of one: female, Black, bilingual.

During the interview with the panel from Foster City, I asked the Lieutenant, "What makes you think the Chief will accept me?" I did not know the Chief from Adam but when the Lieutenant told me that the job was mine if I wanted it, I had to know.

"The Chief gave me the authority to hire on his behalf."

My next statement, "I do not want to be hired because of Affirmative Action."

"No, you are not," he replied. "We heard good things about you and I have all the confidence in the world that you will make the Department proud."

After the interviews, the Administrator asked me if I had made a decision. I told him that I did not know one police agency from another and asked for his advice. He suggested Foster City for several reasons: he knew the Lieutenant, I would be the first woman on the Department, and it's a newly incorporated city with more misdemeanors than felonies.

I returned to the jail and a month later, the Lieutenant called. He offered the job to me again and I accepted. I did not want to leave the Sheriff's Department but working in the jail was not for me.

When I was introduced to the Chief, I noticed that his hand barely touched mine during the hand-shake. Later, I confronted the Lieutenant, "The Chief doesn't like Blacks, does he?"

"Why do you say that?"

"His hand barely touched mine."

"Don't worry about it."

I should have worried. It was a miserable 14 months. The Chief made it clear to the lieutenants and sergeants that he wanted the "nigger" off his depart-ment and threatened to fire the Lieutenant (who hired me) if he didn't get rid of me. The Lieutenant con-sistently gave me applications for other agencies but I tossed them into File 13. Honestly, I was there 10 months before I heard about the Chief's comments. I worked very hard, not to outshine the men but to prove I was their equal.

We rotated shifts every four months. Each shift consisted of a sergeant and two or three patrol officers. About 2 A.M. one morning, while on graveyard shift, the Sergeant gave the code for me to meet him at a certain location. He presented me with a 10-month evaluation which I read, then proceeded to sign. He said, "You can't sign it. The Chief asked me to write your evaluation. I turned this in and he refused to accept it. He told me that I had two days to make it bad. I thought about it and I can't change it. I have to be honest. I just wanted you to see what I wrote."

After this, I could not do anything right. I was placed on swing shift with another sergeant. My reports which were accepted for 10 months were now being returned with red marks, placed there by another lieutenant. When I asked the sergeant what was wrong with the reports, his response was the same, "Nothing. Just rewrite them." In addition, the men would not cover me on traffic stops. Everyone stayed away from me like the plague.

Four months later, I handed in my badge and gun. I returned to Southern California and a year later, applied for jobs with other law enforcement agencies. I passed the physical examinations, made it through the interview process, and was waiting on background checks to be completed. I had a choice between the Inglewood Police Department and the Los Angeles Sheriff's Department.

One day, the mail arrived. Sergeant Steele from Inglewood Police Department sent me a note:

"You have been disqualified from any further consideration with the Inglewood Police Department."

I called him immediately. "Why?" I asked.

"I don't have to tell you anything."

"Would you talk to my attorney?" At the time, I did not have one.

"No, I don't have to tell anyone anything." He hung up on me.

One week later, the phone rang. "Is this Gloria Middleton?"

"Yes."

"Gloria Middleton, you are a liar?"

"Who are you?"

"My name is Deputy O'Neil from the Los Angeles Sheriff's Department. You did not mention that you were fired from the Foster City Department for being a member of the Black Panther's Party?"

Infuriated was not the word. I was shocked, alarmed, exasperated. "Who? What? For your information, I resigned." Then I proceeded to tell him a little about my experiences on the Department: the Chief didn't want a 'nigger' on his Department; no coverage on traffic stops; officers who wouldn't ride in the same police car with me; scratching up my reports and had me rewriting them; trying to get the sergeant to write a negative evaluation..."

"Why didn't you mention that before?"

Nobody asked me and I didn't know they were going to lie."

"I have an evaluation in my hands. It mentioned that you did not follow instructions, that you neglected your duty…"

"Did I sign it?"

"No, but it doesn't matter," was his curt response.

I gave him a couple of names that he could call. I explained that once a month, officers and the sergeant from the Detective Bureau were always at my house. While they enjoyed good cooking of recipes from Besileno, they spent time sharing their law enforcement experiences. I had hoped, one day, to work as a detective since they appeared to be more supportive than the patrol officers. His response was, "The Chief will not lie. We don't hire members of the Black Panther Party." With that he hung up.

Immediately, I contacted the sergeant who had refused to change the evaluation. His reply, "I can't call anyone. The Chief fired me a month after you left for insubordination because I had refused to change the evaluation. Law enforcement was my life."

Mama was working for the O'Sullivan family at the time. I called her and told her what had happened. Her response sent me into a rage. "Just pray. Ask God to forgive him. Don't worry. God doesn't like ugly."

I hung up and screamed. I went to the library and researched the Black Panthers. Two days later, Mama came home for the weekend. I brought up the subject again. Same response, "Leave him to God. Read your Bible. Do not take revenge, my friends, but leave room for God's wrath…"

"I will show him what a Black Panther does. I will march into his office and put a gun in his mouth and pull the trigger."

"Gloria, if you walk out of this house and commit a crime, do not come back here. You will not hide here. I will tell the law man that I told you not to leave this house."

"You know how many mothers would have supported their daughter, and all you can think about is 'read the Bible and pray?'" With that, I stormed out of the house.

I drove around Los Angeles like a mad woman. I was bloody angry. It's my house. What does she mean 'do not come back here?' How could she not understand that the Chief, who was Catholic, had just ruined my chances of ever getting back into law enforcement? He had to be taught a lesson.

For days, weeks, months – as many times as I threatened revenge, I tried to get Mama's support. She did not give an inch. Each time, as I drove North on the 101, I heard Mama's voice, "God says it is mine to avenge. I will repay. Overcome evil with good." In addition, I heard the voices of people in the village where I grew up. They heard about my crime and they had no sympathy for me. "She was so smart around here. She should have stayed here. Went to America and will now be hung." (Besileno was a British commonwealth and the death penalty was administered by hanging.)

Other voices chimed in, "What a disgrace to that sweet family. I can't imagine what her mother is going through."

Yet another added, "She should have stayed in police work right here. She was doing fine, but no, she had to go to America."

Then I heard my father's voice, "It is Ma Dell's fault. She encouraged the kids to leave here. "

*Oh no, I could not let Mama be blamed for my actions. I had to trust God to make things right.*

I attempted four trips to Northern California and each time I heard voices but not one said, "You are doing the right thing." In the end, I gave up. I stayed away from Foster City for twenty years. When I did return it was only to show my sister where I once lived.

I shared this story for several reasons. Mama believed strongly in the Word of God and there are never any good reasons to deviate from them. Mama raised us to do the right thing. Did I have to listen to her? I was my own woman. However, because of the way I was raised, I could not, would not defy Mama.

*Mama, you are truly God's faithful servant. If there is a Heaven, you will be there for sure.*

"I know, O Lord, that a man's life is not his own; it is not for man to direct his steps."

Jer. 10:23 NIV

"Mama, you have been in this world a long time. Looking back, do you have any regrets? Would you have done anything differently?"

"No, I have lived a good life. I have fought a good fight, I have finished my course. I have kept the faith. The Bible says, 'Who is wise and understanding among you, let him show it by his good life, by deeds done in humility that comes from wisdom. A man's life is not his own.' I have followed the teachings of Christ, knowing that he placed me here for a purpose. I had loving parents and a loving family. We were raised to respect and love each other inside and outside of the home. That meant that we helped those in need. We worked hard but that was part of life. If we didn't work, who was going to take care of us? By the sweat of thy brow thou shall eat bread.

"We prayed every morning when we climbed out of bed and we prayed every night before we climbed into bed. There were some tough times - the depression, the hurricanes of 1931 and 1961. We lost a lot but we had each other. People were genuinely good. We helped each other. The hurricanes destroyed several homes so we built them back one at a time. In two weeks, everyone had a shelter over his head. People did not look for repayment. There were no crimes to worry about. There was no stealing and killing like we have today.

"I do miss those days. Children had respect for their elders. The family worked together. The family prayed together. We were always singing gospel songs. We had a roof over our heads. You could sit under a mango tree or a plum tree and eat some fresh fruits.

"It's different here in America. Parents cannot discipline their children. Children don't have respect for their parents, much less anyone else. Crime is everywhere. People seem to care more about material things than about God. I don't know what will become of this world."

"I agree with you, Mama. In those days, the family was always together. There was no television. The lucky families had a radio. You all didn't even have a radio so there was time to talk and listen to each other and spend quality family time."

"Television is the ruination of anything good. Without television, young people would spend more time studying. Where are the parents?"

"Mama, children are having children. They don't know how to be parents. The last three generations of children are lost. Nevertheless, there are a few good programs on television. Mama, it's the parents' responsibility to supervise what their children watch.

But in some families, the children rule. Anyway, I still want to know if you have any regrets."

"No, I lived a good life. I read my Bible everyday and follow God's words. I ask for forgiveness every night for what I may have done or for what I didn't do. I have no regrets. I live every day as if it is my last. He gave me eighty-five good years. My health is good and I can move around. I don't know when He will call me home but when He does, I am ready to stand before God's judgment throne. *'I was upright before Him, and I kept myself from mine iniquity.'* You can find that in the Psalms."

"Mama, I know it's in the Bible. I just can't quote scriptures like you."

Mama smiled and began to sing and I joined in:

> *This world is not my home I'm just a passing through,*
> *If Heaven's not my home, then Lord what will I do?*

*My treasures are laid up somewhere beyond the blue.*

*The angels beckon me from Heaven's open door*

*And I can't feel at home in this world anymore.*

*Oh, Lord you know, I have no friend like you.*

*If Heaven's not my home, then Lord what will I do?*

*The angels beckon me from Heaven's open door*

*And I can't feel at home in this world anymore.*

Dear God,

Thank you for giving us Mama.

She believed in you, and trusted your words,

Challenges or failures did not lessen her faith in you.

She followed your teachings in deeds and in speech;

For that, you rewarded her with a long and fruitful life

And she gave you the glory every single day.

While we don't look forward to losing her

We know that you cannot wait to receive her.

Take her hand and lead her to your throne

Then tell her,

> "Well done, my good and faithful servant.
> Welcome home.
>
> There are no more sorrows, no more fears,

No more burdens, no more tears.

Welcome home, into your Father's arms."

"We love you, Mama. You've done well."

264910BV00001B/1/P

9 781612 155067